D0106147

Don't Go Broke

in a

Nursing Home!

Second Edition

A Consumer's Real-Life, Hands-On Guide To:

- Long-Term Care
- Medicaid Eligibility
- Veterans Benefits for Long-Term Care
- and How to Legally Protect Your Assets

DON QUANTE

AFFC Publications
St. Charles, MO

Don't Go Broke in a Nursing Home!™

This book is being given to

_____

because I care about helping you and your family.

_____

Don't Go Broke in a Nursing Home

For information, please contact Don Quante at *don@donquante.com* or call 1.800.800.6004.

First printing 2011
Second printing 2013
Third printing 2015

PUBLISHED BY:
AFFC Publications
Email: *don@donquante.com*

ISBN: 978-1-4675-0791-2

Attention Coporations, Universities, Colleges, and Professional Organizations: Quantity discounts are available on bulk purchases of this book for educational and/or gift purposes, or as premiums for increasing magazine subscriptions or renewals. Special books or book excerpts can also be created to fit specific needs.

Cover Design and Interior Design by TLC Graphics, *www.tlcgraphics.com*
Cover: Monica Thomas; Interior: Erin Stark
Edited by: Valerie VonBooven and Kee Lawson

CONTRIBUTING AUTHORS:
Rudy D. Beck, Elderlaw Attorney

Dedication

This book is dedicated to the adult children, caregivers, and spouses of aging individuals, and will aid you in all you do to provide quality long-term care for your loved ones. Whether you are caring for a loved one who is confusing the microwave with the oven due to dementia, or you are helping your parent shower and dress each morning, your efforts do not go unnoticed.

This book is also dedicated to the incredible group of elder law attorneys, geriatric care managers and financial advisors who have made it their passion to help families navigate the rough waters as they try to provide quality long-term care for their loved one without going broke in the process.

If you are reading this book, it has most likely been provided to you as a resource from one of these remarkable individuals.

Contents

Acknowledgments

I would like to express my deep sense of gratitude and affection to the people who have had the greatest influence on my personal, professional, and spiritual life in chronological order from their initial impact; my late mother, Barb Quante, for her dogged determination to remind me from the time I was a little boy that you can be anything you want to be if you try hard enough; my father, Don Quante, who modeled for me an incredible work ethic and taught me that a good sense of humor goes a long way; Charlie Costello, my first basketball coach, who taught me that, while winning is important, what's more important is how you play the game; Roy Kassebaum, my first boss, who taught me entrepreneurship; my last official boss, Doug Gritton, who taught me the lesson of being true to one's self; Barb Bott for her never ending administrative, moral and spiritual support over the last 28 years; and lastly, Rudy Beck, my dear friend, business partner, elder law attorney and co-author of this book.

In addition, this book itself could not have happened the way that it has without the unique energies and perspectives of Erin Stark, Monica Thomas and the great people at TLC Graphics. Much credit is due to my editor, Valerie VanBooven, who has been a marvelous and patient instructor with regard to the art and craft of book writing.

My deepest thanks and love go out to my wonderful children Jessica, Ryan and Allison for being so supportive and tolerating my incredibly long hours away from home. And last but not least to my wife, Sheila, for her trust, love, hard work and the beauty and joy she has brought into my life. Without her holding things together at home, none of our success would've been possible.

Don Quante

Lottie's Million Dollar Story

"If I only knew then what I know now." It's a phrase that most of us will use at least once—perhaps hundreds of times—as we age. We face a new situation with little knowledge and much trepidation and inevitably, we discover that there was a better way to handle things.

Such was the case in my own experience with my grandmother. The year was 1983, and I was a little wet behind the ears in my new career as a financial planner. I was working at a large financial services firm in St. Louis, and though I had received the best training available in the industry from that company, I was completely unprepared for what my own family was about to go through.

A year later, my grandma—Lottie Holton—was diagnosed with Alzheimer's Disease. Although, at the time, Grandma was only in the early stages of the disease, the doctor had told my mom that there was no way to tell how long she would be safe at home. In other words, there were decisions to be made and not a lot of time to make them.

Deciding how my Grandma would be cared for was no small task. We needed to figure out what kind of care she would need, how we would pay for that care and whether we had the legal authority to act on her behalf.

This is a dilemma many adult children face when mom or dad suffers a heart attack or stroke, takes an unexpected fall, or in my grandma's case, is diagnosed with an ultimately fatal disease. Furthermore, these adult children are often totally unprepared to answer the questions they are soon to face on a personal and financial level.

"How much did mom and dad make while we were growing up?" and "How much is left?" are some of the best kept secrets we learn as they age.

In my family's case, we called two or three attorneys in the St. Louis area. They all said the same thing, "There's not much you can do except spend the money down to the threshold allowed by federal law." That federal law dictates that the maximum an individual can have before qualifying for Medicaid in a vendor bed at a nursing home is $2,000 in most states, and $999.99 in Missouri, which is where I live.

So once an individual in Missouri has one penny short of $1,000 to their name, the government will pay the cost of the nursing home over and above their pension and Social Security.

That would have been sound advice back then, but they did not tell us the whole story. There were other things we could have done to make the money last twice as long, such as set up a medicaid compliant annuity. The Federal government tells you that you can take countable assets—those things federal law says you must spend down, including savings, checking accounts, Certificates of Deposit, IRA's, stocks, bonds etc.—and put them into a medicaid compliant annuity.

While many people have annuities, in order for an annuity to be considered not countable it must comply with OBRA '93. This law states that if an annuity meets the following criteria, it will not be counted as an asset:

1. It must be irrevocable.
2. It must be non-assignable.
3. It must be non-commutable.
4. It must be non-transferable.
5. It must be actuarially sound.

The one thing most of us would rather avoid than discuss is the topic of long-term care. The need for long-term care can cause tremendous devastation to individuals and families, and is the number one reason why people outlive their money.

Our family did discuss all of the options, and our first choice was to move Grandma in with Mom and Dad. After all, Mom was her daughter and they had the room. As time went on, however, the burden became greater and greater. My younger brother and sister were still at home, making it necessary for Mom and Dad to deal with the balancing act of worrying whether Grandma would wander off in addition to raising teenage children.

After that, Grandma went through a series of nursing homes as we struggled to find the best place for her and us. By 1986, half of her money had been spent on care. After seven years and seven months, she had outlived her money. My grandma Lottie, who had worked her entire life in a shoe factory and saved over $120,000 for her retirement, died broke in a nursing home.

This was something I vowed would never happen again in my family, not to my parents or to myself. That was when Wealth Protection Advisors was born. Wealth Protection Advisors is a boutique financial planning firm that works exclusively with baby-boomers to secure quality, long-term care for their parents without going broke in the process. As a result, we have helped over 3700 families and trained over 1800 advisors to help their clients with long-term care planning strategies.

Wealth Protection Advisors exists because of Lottie Holton. She worked hard and saved all of the tin foil and re-used plastic storage bags. When she retired, she had about $120,000 saved and a comfortable pension. Unfortunately, because of poor planning, 100% of her assets were depleted in approximately seven years.

As we began examining the family's situation, we attempted to answer the question, "Was the real cost of her care $120,000?" We figured that if we had been able to take the $120,000 and invest it in the bull market (and could have taken advantage of the tremendous growth in our economy) from 1983 to 2000, Lottie's money would have grown in excess of $1,000,000! Had we handled things differently, Grandma would still have been in a nursing home, would still have occupied a Medicaid bed, but could have passed her life savings on to her two daughters.

It is this fact that has taught me how devastating it can be for families who have loved ones who need care. In fact, most of the folks who work in our office have a personal story about someone in their family who has needed long-term care and you are most likely reading this book because you have too.

By understanding what the federal and state law would have legally allowed, we could have protected in excess of $120,000 and Lottie could have realized her dream of leaving her children with a sizable inheritance. If we had known how to legally protect my Grandma's money, she would have received the same quality of care, but her assets would have remained virtually intact to be passed on to the next generation, which was her intent.

The implication of my story is that our previous planning cost my family in excess of $1,000,000. My only question is: how much in excess would it have been? Unfortunately, we will never know. As a financial planner, I should have known better.

Instead, we took a case worker's word that we had to spend down my Grandma's assets. Again, that was only half of the story; technically, we did have to spend down Lottie's assets, but they had not been candid about what to spend it on. Did it have to be on the care of the person? As it turns out, that is not altogether true.

The State of Missouri Maintenance Manual states exactly what you can spend assets on, one of which is a medicaid compliant annuity. Most states allow the medicaid compliant annuity.

Now, most people reading this book probably have a financial advisor, whether it be a banker, stock broker, analyst, or whomever you rely on to teach you how to manage and increase your money. However, like me in 1984, unless this individual has special training and has dedicated his or her work to asset protection planning, you may not be getting the best advice.

There are several financial planning strategies we could have used to protect my Grandma's money and the next generation, her two daughters, would have had in excess of $1,000,000 today.

The lack of good, quality financial advice on the topic of long-term care planning is what caused me to create the hundreds of workshops my firm has held in the last eleven years on the topic in hospitals, senior centers, independent living facilities, libraries and nursing homes across the United States. It is what causes me to appear on talk and radio shows and why I was compelled to write this book.

As a grandchild and a financial planner, I clearly failed my family by not offering them sound advice in this area. The moral of the story is that if you have someone in this situation, pay attention to the next two sections of this book very carefully. Whether you are meeting a family crisis today or looking ahead to make sure you do not face such a crisis in the future, the information contained herein is for adult children and their parents and may keep you and them from going broke in a nursing home.

Don Quante

The Long-Term Care Crisis

A Close Look at the Numbers: The Cost of Care

The biggest and most obvious question for seniors and for long-term care needs is usually money. How are we going to pay for long-term care?

According to Genworth* in 2015 the cost of care looks like this:

- The national average daily rate for a private room in a nursing home is $250 while the daily rate for a semi-private room is $220, an increase of 4% from 2014.

- The national average monthly base rate in an assisted-living community rose to $3,600, increasing 3% from 2014

- The national average hourly rate for home health aides is $20; for homemakers it is $20. The national average daily rate for adult day services is $65.

The 2015 Genworth Cost of Care Survey; Home Care Providers, Adult Day Health Care Facilities, Assisted Living Facilities and Nursing Homes

Privately paying for long-term care means that seniors would have to find an additional $40,000 to $130,000 per year in their budget for just ONE person to receive care. Most of us, seniors or not, could not afford to privately pay for our own care year after year.

Long-term care insurance will pay for in-home care, assisted living, and nursing-home care. This is the most appropriate and needed form of insurance protection available to us today. Long-term care insurance should be termed "lifestyle" insurance—it is NOT nursing-home insurance! If your vision of your later years includes sitting at home in your own recliner, with your own remote control, watching your own TV…well, you should be planning for that future with long-term care insurance. In later chapters we discuss all of the options related to long-term care insurance today.

Reverse mortgages (Home Equity Conversion Mortgages) have become one of the most popular and accepted ways of paying for many different expenses, including the cost of long-term care. Reverse mortgages are designed to keep seniors at home longer. A reverse mortgage can pay for in-home care, home repair, home modification, and any other need a senior may have. Almost every successive chapter in this book discusses the use of reverse mortgages for seniors in some way. That is how important this cash flow planning concept has become in recent years.

Government Assistance

Medicaid will pay for long-term care, but certain criteria must be met. It is important to seek the advice of a qualified financial professional and an elder law attorney prior to applying for Medicaid.

VA Aid and Attendance Pension Benefit: The VA Aid and Attendance Pension Benefit is available to certain Veterans and their spouses who served during a period of war. Both Medicaid and VA Aid and Attendance are discussed later in the book.

Who Is Going to Take Care of Mom and Dad?

According to a recent joint study conducted by Cornell and Purdue University and supported by the National Institute on Aging, aging mothers are nearly four times more likely to expect a daughter to assume the role of their caregiver rather than a son if they become ill or disabled.

These mothers are also much more likely to choose a child to whom they feel emotionally close and who has values similar to their own, according to Karl Pillemer, Professor of Human Development at Cornell, and Purdue sociologist Jill Suitor, in the journal, "The Gerontologist".[1]

Aging adults today who are on the threshold of needing additional assistance in the home are also aging adults who tended to have larger families during their childbearing years. It is important, though often difficult, for seniors to talk with their adult children about expectations and wishes. It is also important for adult children to talk with each other about who will be assuming what role with regard to helping Mom and Dad. Neglecting to discuss this at all can lead to disappointment, confusion and disagreement between siblings.

Long-term care is a family issue, but it is more often a woman's issue. Throughout history women have been the caregivers in our lives. As we have seen, women also live longer than men on average. From beginning to end, women often care for family members young and old. Now, as our population begins to age, it is even more important that we understand what lies before us.

Although we see the number of male caregivers increasing all the time, the fact remains that, when it comes to long-term care for our family members and our spouses, today women carry the weight.

Daughters, daughters-in-law, wives, sisters and nieces often accept the role of caregiver for aging adults in the family. Across the U.S. there are women commonly referred to as "the sandwich generation" who are playing dual roles in their families. They are often mothers themselves in addition to caring for their own aging parents. The level of stress and frustration can be overwhelming. Careers are being put on hold, and promotions passed up, in order to accommodate the busy schedules of their children, and their parents. Even so, there is still not enough time for these women to meet everyone's needs. A financial burden results as well.

Women in America also tend to marry men who are older than they are. Therefore, they often end up caring for a chronically ill spouse in later years. When this happens, it is sometimes the case that all of the retirement funding and assets are used to pay for the long-term care needs of the "ill" spouse, leaving nothing in savings to care for the "well" spouse later in life.

It is estimated that one out of every two women will need long-term care at some point in their lives. One of every three men will also require long-term care. So why do more women need services? A woman's life expectancy is still longer than that of the average male.

How Long Can Seniors Be Cared for at Home—Realistically?

The answer to this question depends on many things, but ultimately it depends on how much support seniors have in their own community from family, friends, neighbors and religious organizations, and their ease of access to the medical system. Cash flow, as previously discussed, is another factor that determines how long seniors can stay at home safely.

It is important to note that according to a study by the National Association of Home Builders 50 + Housing Council, for those owning single family homes, 35.9 % of households in the 55 to 64 age group reported difficulty in at least one physical activity:

- difficulty in dressing (9 %)
- vision or hearing difficulty (11 %)
- difficulty in going out (11.9 %)
- difficulty in walking, reaching, lifting, carrying, climbing stairs or getting around the house (27.1 %)
- difficulty in remembering (12.7 %)
- and difficulty in working (23.8 %)

More than 45 % of those 65 to 74 and 70 % of households 75 or older reported difficulty in some activity.[2]

Set up properly, a senior can stay in his or her own home for their entire life. As long as care can be paid for, or provided by family members locally, and as long as the living situation is safe and comfortable, seniors can stay at home. In the next few chapters we will give you more information on how this can be achieved.

References

[1] *The Gerontologist* 46:439-448 (2006) © 2006 The Gerontological Society of America Making Choices: A Within-Family Study of Caregiver Selection Karl Pillemer, PhD1, and J. Jill Suitor, PhD

[2] March 2007, National Association of Home Builders 50 + Housing Council Study—Aging Boomers May Be Hard to Budge From Current Homes

CHAPTER TWO

Where Will Your Aging Parent Receive Care?

Choosing the Right Home Care Agency

he most desirable choice for many families is to keep an aging loved one at home for as long as possible. Assuming that is the case, here are some tips on choosing a home care agency.

- Be organized.
- Ask the Home Care Agency if they have a back-up person on call in case of caregivers becoming ill or not showing up.
- Provide the aide with a checklist of duties for EACH DAY.
- The aide should not sleep or smoke in your home.
- If there is a problem, immediately contact the agency that sent the aide.
- The aides should provide their own lunch/dinner unless you offer.
- Do not tip.
- Do not send your loved one out in a car with the aide unless this situation is prearranged with the agency.

- Aides should only minimally use the phone for personal calls.
- Make sure you know in advance how payment is expected.
- Some aides are Certified Nurse's Aides (CNAs) and others are not. Some will take a blood pressure and a pulse, while others will not. Ask the agency.
- There should be some consistency after about 1 to 2 weeks regarding the person who is sent to the home. Sometimes it takes a week or so to get the same person on the schedule for your home. Be patient!
- What is the hiring practice of the agency? Have background checks been performed on every caregiver? What about Elder Abuse or Child Abuse database checks? Are they bonded and insured?
- If there are too many late shows/no shows or inconsistencies, CHANGE AGENCIES (speak to them about the problem first, perhaps they can correct the situation).

Medical vs. Non-Medical Home Care Services

There are two different types of home-care providers, **medical** and **non-medical**. A non-medical home-care agency supplies caregivers who will do household chores such as light cleaning, laundry, errand running, grocery shopping, picking up prescriptions, light meal preparation and getting the mail. They will also provide services that help with socialization and transportation like accompanying the aging adult to a doctor's appointment, sitting and watching TV together, playing card games or board games, taking the senior to special events or senior centers, going to the library, and other social activities. Again, transporting the senior in the caregiver's vehicle should be pre-approved.

In addition, non-medical home-care providers can also provide bathing and dressing assistance, medication reminders, and assistance with transferring from the bed to a chair. Medical home-care provides physical, occupational and speech therapy as well as wound care.

No one can take care of your parent or spouse exactly the way you would, but a good agency will provide caring and compassionate staff who do the best job they possibly can. The squeaky wheel always gets the grease when it comes to service providers. Do your homework prior to hiring an agency, and be sure to check on your aging loved one regularly. Visit unexpectedly and monitor what is happening in the home. Speak up and communicate with the agency!

Choosing an Adult Day Services Center

Adult day care centers are becoming a popular alternative to nursing home placement. They offer the ability for the elderly to spend the day in an enriching environment, full of social activities and learning opportunities, while interacting with others. Many adult day care centers will provide transportation to and from the center for an extra charge. Meals are provided, as well as medication administration. Day trips, crafts, computer stations, libraries and music are often part of the overall experience. Some adult day care centers will take Medicaid, but most prefer private pay or long-term care insurance. This allows the senior to live at home with another member of the family, but have supervision and social interaction during the day while family members are at work.

Tips for Choosing an Adult Day Services Center

- *Identify services in your area.* For names and phone numbers of the adult day care centers, try:
  - *Yellow Pages* ("Adult Day Care;" "Aging Services;" Senior Citizens' Services," etc.).

- *Area Agency on Aging (AAA)*. Call 1-800-677-1116 for the AAA in your area, or search for them online.

  • *A local senior center.*

  • *Your family doctor.*

  • *A Geriatric Care Manager.*

* *Call first!* Call adult day care centers and ask for a flier or brochure, eligibility criteria, a monthly activity calendar, a monthly menu and application procedures.

* *Know what to ask.* Look for the following information:

  - *Owner or sponsoring agency.*

  - *Years of operation.*

  - *Openings and availability.* Are they accepting new clients?

  - *License or certification* (if required in your state).

  - *Hours of operation.*

  - *Days open.*

  - *Transportation.*

  - *Cost.* Hourly or daily charge, other charges, financial assistance.

  - *Medical conditions accepted.* Such as memory loss, limited mobility, and incontinence.

  - *Staff credentials.*

  - *Number of staff per participant.*

  - *Activities provided.* Is there variety and choice of individual and group activities?

  - *Menu.* Appeal, balance.

  - *Tour.* After reviewing materials, make an appointment to visit two or more centers that might meet your needs.

  - *Check references.* Talk to two or three people who have used the center you are considering. Ask for their opinion.

– *Try it out.* Select a day center. Try it for three to five days. It sometimes takes several visits for new participants to feel comfortable in a new setting and with a new routine. If you have questions or are experiencing any problems, ask for a conference. The staff may have suggestions for making the transition easier, both at home and at the day center.

Choosing an Assisted-Living Facility

Sometimes there are assisted-living facilities on the same campus that offer most of the same accommodations, but with a little more assistance and structure. In an assisted-living facility, each resident typically has their own apartment, but without a kitchenette. They are served three meals per day in a family-style or restaurant-style setting. Medication delivery is available, as well as linen service, laundry service, housekeeping, and assistance with bathing and dressing if needed. Again, recreation, social activities and transportation are also provided.

There are stand-alone assisted-living facilities that are not associated with Continuous Care Retirement Communities (CCRCs). Assisted living is becoming the most popular form of long-term care, and is seen as a transition between independent living and nursing-home care. This is a nice option for people who need some extra help but are not ready for full 24-hour care. The cost of assisted-living ranges from $1900-$5000 per month and can be paid for with private funds or long-term care insurance. Occasionally in some states assisted-living facilities can accept Medicaid.

Nursing Home Care

When independent or assisted living is no longer a viable option, a nursing home will provide 24-hour care by trained and licensed staff. A Registered Nurse or Licensed Practical Nurse is on duty at all times. Some nursing homes are private pay only, some take Medicare, and some will accept Medicaid as payment for services. Most residents live in a semi-private room (private if they can afford it), and are allowed to decorate with their own personal belongings. There are new trends in nursing-home care called The Eden Alternative ™. These programs incorporate living things like plants, animals and children into residential care facilities to make them more like a home, rather than an institution for the frail and elderly. The average cost for a semi-private nursing home bed nationwide in 2014 was around $212 per day ($6,448 per month) or more.

Tips for Choosing an Assisted-Living or Nursing-Care Facility

Choosing a facility for a loved one, or even for yourself, can be difficult and time-consuming. The following tips and hints will help give you guidance when trying to make that decision. Remember—take notes on each facility you visit and compare them later. Anticipating your loved one's need for nursing home care will be very important, especially if your loved one has dementia, since many dementia units have waiting lists that can range from 6 to 18 months.

- Speak with people you trust about their experiences with nursing homes.
- Pick a good LOCATION.
- Ask the home about BED AVAILABILITY.
- Do they have Medicare, Medicaid, or private pay beds available?
- What is the STAFFING ARRANGMENT? RNS? LPNS? CNAS?

- Are there extra services and fees?
- Is the home able to provide for special care needs such as Alzheimer's, End Stage Renal Disease, or other medical conditions?
- VISIT THE HOMES ON YOUR LIST! Nothing replaces a tour.
- Ask to see a copy of the most recent state inspection, or visit the Nursing Home Compare site on the web at *www.medicare.gov.*
- Do the residents seem to have a good quality of life?
- How long has the current staff been working at the facility?
- Does the facility conduct background checks for criminal and elder abuse activity prior to hiring employees?
- Upon entering the facility, pay attention to what you SEE and what you SMELL.
- What are the visiting hours?
- Security? Safety plans for fire evacuations etc.?
- Be sure to visit the home at least once when they are not expecting you.
- Make an inventory of the items that you or your loved one bring to the home for future reference. It would also be a good idea to label everything, such as canes, wheelchair, walker, etc.
- Talk to some of the other visitors/family members. How do they feel about the care provided?

CHAPTER THREE

Adult Children and Family Members Caring for an Aging Adult—Give Yourself a Break

When the Caregiver Needs a Break... Where Can They Turn?

One out of every four families in the U.S. today are caring for an aging adult in some way. For some families, that means 24-hour live-in care. For other families, that means that mom needs a ride to the doctor or to the grocery store.

In the next 10-20 years, it is projected that elder care will replace childcare as the number one issue for working adults. Employers will likewise be affected.

Caring for an aging parent can be rewarding and overwhelming at the same time. After all, these are one's parents who raised and cared for us. It is very difficult when the roles reverse.

Respite (*res*-pit) care is often the answer. Respite care is *time off* for the caregiver. Respite gives the caregiver time away to rest and do necessary activities so that they can continue to provide good care for their loved one. Being a caregiver is often a job that can be physically and emotionally draining. Without relief, a person's physical and emotional health can be affected, reducing the quality of care for their family member. There are several options when it comes to respite care.

In-home care can be arranged for as little as a few hours, up to several days with the proper planning and financial resources. Be sure to pick an agency with a great reputation and proven reliability. Make sure that background checks are done on all employees and Elder/Child Abuse checks are also completed. In-home care for long periods of time can be costly, so be sure to budget for the expense. Also many home health agencies require several days or weeks of advance notice for long assignments. Plan ahead!

Nursing-Care/Assisted-Living facilities will often offer respite care for a weekend or a full week or more. Many facilities have a minimum number of days required. The cost includes room and board; many other services will be extra. Some facilities will only require a few day's notice, and others will require several week's notice. Check with the facilities in your area for costs and bed availability. As always, it is important to plan ahead.

Local Area Agencies on Aging or Social Service Agencies will sometimes sponsor programs that allow for volunteers to come to the home and provide respite care for short periods of time. These visits are usually just for a few hours. The volunteers are not medical professionals and therefore are not able to care for seriously ill family members, but they are able to provide some relief! These programs are usually free or at a very low cost to local residents. Contact your local Area Agency on Aging for more information.

The **Alzheimer's Association** is a great source of information. It is not necessary to be taking care of an Alzheimer's-diagnosed family member to take advantage of their referral database. Your local agency can usually provide you with a wealth of information, resources and contacts.

Family and friends are a great resource for the caregiver. Do not be afraid to ask for help; many people are happy to assist with errand running and caregiving. Have a family meeting and ask each family member for 1-2 hours of his or her time per week; this will allow the caregiver to take a hot bath, read a book, go for a much-needed walk, or just go shopping. Make a schedule and give each family member a copy.

Local Churches and Other Organizations are generally willing to send volunteers out to the home for a few hours. Again, most of these volunteers are non-medical personnel and will only be able to stay for a couple of hours at a time.

Taking care of yourself is just as important as caring for your disabled/aging family member. If you become ill, what will happen to your loved one? Do not hesitate to ask for help. If you look in the right places, you might find more help than you need.

So take a much-needed break. You deserve it!

Hospice Care—at the End of Life

Hospice care is end-of-life care. Usually, it is estimated by a physician that a patient has 6 months or less to live. Hospice focuses on caring for the individual, keeping them comfortable, and providing support for the family. Hospice care can be provided in the home, in a designated hospice facility, or in a long-term care facility. These services are available to patients of all ages. It is covered under Medicare, Medicaid, and most private insurance plans. Long-term care insurance also covers hospice care.

The primary caregiver for a hospice patient is usually a family member. There is a team of healthcare professionals available to help the primary caregiver; this team often includes a physician, a registered nurse, home health aides, clergy or social services, trained volunteers, and physical or occupational therapists. Traditional insurance plans like Medicare and private health insurance will cover needed supplies, equipment, and licensed healthcare practitioners like nurses and physical therapists. However, when a family needs 24 hour care provided by a home health aide, or other unlicensed personnel, they end up paying privately for this service or utilizing their long-term care insurance benefits. Most long-term care insurers provide hospice care as a standard benefit in their plan and there is no need to meet the waiting period (elimination period).

Pay Yourself or a Loved One for Providing Care— The Options and Tax Benefits

Many adult children find it financially impossible to leave their current employer and give up a much needed salary to take care of an aging adult. There are some ways to offset that financial responsibility, but it does take diligence and investigation on the part of the adult child.

Seniors can pay adult children or other care providers, just like they would a home health agency for services, by using a caregiver's contract. This document can be drafted by an elder law attorney.

Some seniors have long-term care insurance that allows a family member to be the primary caregiver, and get reimbursed for providing the care.

If neither of those options apply, here are some other options:

- If employed, check with your company's human resource department or seek the counsel of your employee assistance program to find out about family leave options or local programs that assist with caregiving expenses and options.
- Contact Eldercare Locator, a service of the National Association of Area Agencies on Aging at *www.n4a.org/locator* or phone 800-677-1116.
- A state-by-state listing of paid leave programs for caregivers can be found at *www.paidfamilyleave.org*

Some other examples that offer at least some level of compensation for caregiving family members include:

- *Colorado:* in rural areas, family members providing assistance to loved ones may be eligible to receive up to $400 per month as compensation for providing personal care services.
- *North Dakota:* pays up to $700 per month to spouses and other family members who care for Medicaid beneficiaries living in rural areas who would otherwise require admission to a nursing home.
- *Wisconsin:* a family member may be eligible for compensation either for caregiving, or in some situations, for performing services normally provided by a social worker.
- *North Carolina:* family caregivers supporting loved ones may be able to reduce out of pocket expenses through the use of state-funded vouchers that can be used to buy nutritional supplements, incontinence supplies, and personal emergency response systems, among other items. In some circumstances, caregivers may be eligible for direct cash compensation. While in most cases compensation is pro-

vided to family members who are not immediate family, there are times when immediate family is eligible for pay, such as when they are caring for a loved one with dementia who lives in a rural area.

* *Massachusetts:* elders who meet Medicaid criteria and who qualify for nursing-home care now have the option of receiving compensated home-based care from family members or friends. The Enhanced Adult Foster Program covers up to $18,000 annually for family members who provide 24-hour care in the home. These caregivers receive specialized training, support of both a registered nurse and a care manager, and help in locating respite services.

Tax Deductions and Benefits for Caregivers

There are certain criteria that must be met if a family caregiver is planning to claim an aging parent as a dependent.

1. You must provide more than half of a person's financial support.

2. The dependent may be a relative or non-relative living with you for the entire year or residing in a nursing home or assisted-living home.

3. The dependent must be a citizen of the U.S., Canada, or Mexico.

4. The dependent must not file a joint tax return for the same year.

Qualifying expenses include:

1. medications
2. long-term care insurance premiums
3. home modifications
4. transportation for medical appointments
5. services of privately hired in-home care workers
6. spending for wheelchairs, eye glasses, and dentures
7. Look for anything related to meeting the long-term care needs of the individual! Any expense not covered by insurance may be eligible for deductions.
8. For those residing in an assisted-living facility, there may be a certain percentage allowed as deductions.
9. For those residing in a nursing home—and paying privately for their care, the cost is fully deductible.

It is important to consult a tax advisor or elder law attorney, especially if the support gets complicated—for instance:

* When multiple siblings contribute to the support of a parent.
* When taxable income could be moved into tax-free investments.
* When there is the possibility that the dependent may need to apply for Medicaid.
* When a caregiver contract is desired to provide family members with compensation for services, housing, etc.

If you hired someone to care for your loved one while you either sought or maintained employment, you may qualify for the Child and Dependent Care Credit. Depending on your income, this credit may equal up to 35% of your qualifying expenses. To claim the credit, the following conditions must be met:

* You must have earned income wages, salaries, tips, employee compensation, or net earnings from self-employment.
* Payments for care cannot be made to any person you claim as a dependent, or to your child under age 19.
* You must file as single, head of household, qualified widow(er) with a dependent child, or married filing jointly.
* The care must have been provided by a qualifying individual.
* The dependent must have lived with you for more than half of the year.

Remember to consult a local tax consultant for more help, information, and possible state level deductions in your area.

Talk to Employers about Dependent Care FSAs

Consider utilizing a Dependent Care FSA (Flexible Spending Accounts) to help pay for medical/elder care expenses. These plans allow employees to contribute a portion of salary, before taxes, to accounts designated for health care expenses, including premiums and child/elder care expenses. Then employees are reimbursed from their accounts with tax free dollars for unreimbursed medical expenses and child/elder care expenses. The funds must be used before the end of the plan year, or grace period, or else unused dollars are forfeited. If a caregiver has access to these plans, they should use them, but plan carefully so that contributions are not more than can be used in a year.

If an elderly parent lives with a participant and relies on that person for at least 50 % of their support, then the Dependent Care FSA may be used for day care expenses. However, the care must be necessary to allow the participant to work, and cannot be custodial nursing care. Also, if the participant is married, the care must be necessary because the spouse also works, is looking for work, or is a full-time student.

Common (Partial) Solutions to the Long-Term Care Crisis

CHAPTER FOUR

Safety in the Home

How Can We Keep Seniors Safe in Their Own Home?

Keeping seniors safe includes making sure that the interior and exterior of the home is up-to-code, senior friendly, and accessible for those who are disabled. Interior safety includes modifications such as safety grab bars in the bathrooms, elevated toilet seats, and lower sink and vanity heights if needed. Kitchen cabinets can be lowered for easier accessibility. Doorways in older homes may be too narrow for walkers and wheelchairs, and may need to be widened if possible. Levered door handles are a plus for everyone. Throw rugs are a bad idea in a senior's home; they contribute to falls more often than not. On the exterior of the home, there should be sturdy handrails wherever there are steps or uneven pavement. Senior friendly homes are now constructed on one level with no steps at the front door or garage entry. Many home builders are now specialized in senior living and are available for consultation. For a list of contractors, you can go to *www.AgingInPlace.com*.

Personal Emergency Response Systems

Personal emergency response systems (PERS) are another form of safety that should always be considered. A "PERS" is a system that can be set up very inexpensively in a senior's home. This is not just for "sick" people; these systems keep well people well. The senior wears a pendant around their neck, or a watch style pendant, and has the system with them at all times inside and outside of the house. If they suffer a fall, stroke, illness, or any other event where they feel they might need assistance, all they have to do is access their system with the touch of a button.

Statistics

- A study by AC Nielson indicates among other things that seniors who have a personal emergency response system **stay at home an average of 6 years longer** than those who do not have a PERS. Also, most PERS have smoke detector options, keeping the home safe and protected from fire devastation.

- 58 % of customers who have had a PERS for a year or more feel that their quality of life has improved.

- 87 % of customers with a PERS think that this protection is important or a main factor in their decision to continue living at home.

- 95 % of customers with a PERS feel protected at home.

- 80 % feel that the comfort of living in their own home is important.

- 76 % feel that being independent is important.

- **In a study of older adults, those living with a PERS reported significantly greater ability to go about their daily routine and were *ten times* less likely to require admission to a nursing home.**

- Medical research shows that falling down and being unable to get help is not an uncommon event. In fact, nearly *1/3* of all people over the age of 65 (and *half* of all people over 90) will fall each year. Of course, the older a senior gets, the more dangerous and debilitating falls can be, and they often mark the end of independent living.

- Research also tells us that 30% to 50% of elderly people fear falling—a fear that can cause them to lose confidence and restrict their normal range of healthy activities. The confidence and peace-of-mind that comes from a PERS helps to ease these anxieties, as well as the feelings of isolation and depression caused by such worries.

Facts about Personal Emergency Response Systems

- **PERS are recommended by doctors, nurses and other professional caregivers.** They know even a minor fall or incident can have serious physical and psychological consequences if a senior cannot get help in a hurry.

- **A PERS is for independent living at home.** The alternative to getting a PERS is often assisted living, a nursing home, or 24-hour care.

- **A PERS is a good idea even if a senior does not live alone.** Accidents are unpredictable; a senior might need help when someone they live with is temporarily out of the house.

- **A PERS is easy to live with.** The personal help button is very small, simple to use and will not interfere with a senior's activities in any way.

- **A PERS is for everyday living.** A PERS telephone also includes many other features that makes conversing with others more convenient, and can provide personalized reminders of important things to do.

CHAPTER FIVE

Understanding Health Insurance and Medicare:
Does Medicare Pay for Long-Term Care?

"I'm Already Covered, Right?"

There is a common misconception about health insurance paying for the cost of long-term care; health insurance, including Medicare, Medicare Supplements, HMOs, private insurance through employers, and disability insurance, was never designed to pay for the cost of long-term care.

Medicare and Other Health Insurances

Medicare is a federal health insurance program for people 65 and older, certain people with disabilities, and those with ESRD (End Stage Renal Disease). It pays for much of your health care, but not all of it; there are some costs you will have to pay yourself. (*www.medicare.gov*)

There are other kinds of health insurance that may help pay the costs that Medicare does not; Medicare Supplements (Medigap Policies) and long-term care insurance will pick up some of the costs that Medicare will not pay for.

Medicare was implemented in 1965. How many times has Medicare been over-hauled since 1965? NEVER. It was not designed to pay for care related to diseases or conditions such as Alzheimer's disease, Parkinson's, or MS. The average life expectancy was much lower in 1965 because medical technology was not as advanced. Medicare was designed for SHORT-TERM, acute care, and short-term, rehabilitative stays in a rehab or long-term care facility. Although Medicare Part D was added in 2004/2005 to help with the costs of prescription drugs, Medicare still does not pay for long-term care.

What Will Medicare Pay?

Medicare comes in four parts; medicare Part A, Part B, Part C, and now Part D for prescription drugs.

Medicare Part A is Hospital Insurance.

Part A pays for inpatient hospital care, some skilled nursing-facility care, hospice care, and some home health care. Most people get Medicare Part A automatically when they turn 65. There is usually no premium or monthly payment for Part A.

Medicare Part B is Medical Insurance.

Part B pays for doctor services, outpatient hospital care, and some other medical services that Part A does not pay for. Part B pays for these services and supplies when they are medically necessary. Part B has a premium that changes every year.

What Will Medicare A and B NOT Pay For?

Medicare carries some high deductibles. For instance, in 2015, during a hospital stay you will automatically have a $1,260 total deductible for days 1-60; on day 61 you are responsible for $315 (your deductible) per day through day 90; on day 91 you pay $630 per day (your deductible) through day 150. This amounts to a substantial out-of-pocket expense for the Medicare recipient.

For a skilled nursing facility stay, Medicare pays for days 1-20; on day 21 you pay $157.50 deductible through day 100. Beyond 101 days you are responsible for all costs.

Also, you will be responsible for 20 % for most covered services under Part B, 50 % for outpatient mental health treatment, and a co-pay for outpatient hospital services.

Medicare was never designed to pay for long-term care. In other words, if you will be living in a nursing home or if you will need around-the-clock care at home, Medicare does not pay for these services. Medicare is for acute, short-term medical care and rehabilitative care only, otherwise called "skilled care."

Defining Skilled Care vs. Custodial Care

Skilled care is defined as care that is prescribed by a physician and performed by a licensed health care professional, such as a nurse, physical therapist, or occupational therapist. Some examples of skilled care include: some wound care, IV antibiotics, or physical therapy immediately after a stroke.

Custodial care is another term for privately paid care. This type of care can be performed by home health aides or other unlicensed caregivers, such as family members. Some examples of custodial care include bathing, dressing, transferring from the bed to a chair, or toileting.

A Medicare Supplement policy will only cover some or all of the deductibles described above. This is a policy that you will have to purchase separately. Medicare supplements will not pay for (custodial) long-term care costs; they simply cover the deductibles under Medicare and sometimes pay for a few extras.

Long-term care insurance will not cover Medicare deductibles like a Medicare Supplement policy will, but long-term care insurance will pay for all of the costs associated with long-term (custodial) nursing-home care, in-home care, assisted living, and adult day care.

Medicare Supplements

Medicare supplements, often referred to as Medigap plans, are purchased through private insurance companies to help fill the "gaps" that Medicare leaves behind. Medicare supplements pick up the co-pays and deductibles associated with standard Medicare. There are ten standardized plans available labeled A, B, C, D, F, G, K, L, M, N. Each plan has a different set of benefits. Medicare supplements also do not cover the cost of long-term care; they simply pay deductibles and co-pays that Medicare does not.

Medicare HMOs
(a.k.a. Medicare Advantage or Medicare+Choice)

HMOs are health maintenance organizations. An HMO will require that the participant use certain doctors and hospital systems in their area. HMOs are also for short, acute care stays in hospitals, and for short, rehabilitative stays in skilled nursing facilities. They do not pay for the cost of long-term care.

Private Insurance

Private health insurance through an employer or previous employer is essentially the same as an HMO as far as coverage. Standard health insurance, no matter how great the benefit, will ultimately fail to cover long-term care.

Disability Insurance

Disability insurance covers household expenses, and is designed as income replacement. It will pay for things like groceries, rent and utilities. This insurance was not designed to cover the added expense of long-term care.

CHAPTER SIX

Understanding Medicaid

Medicaid Defined

Medicaid was established by federal law (Title XIX of the Social Security Act), and is administered by each state individually. Medicaid is a program for poor or "impoverished" people and people with high medical costs. Congress established Medicaid to provide a "safety net" for people who had no other way to pay for their health care or long-term care.

Medicaid is the long-term care payer of last resort for the frail elderly, persons with health problems, persons with mental retardation or mental illness, and those with physical or developmental disabilities.

Most long-term care and services, such as prescription drugs, eyeglasses and dental care, are provided at each state's discretion. When state money is scarce, these services may be the most vulnerable, not because of ill will on the part of the state decision makers, but because there may be nowhere else to cut state budgets.

Medicaid is a highly flawed program, and is under-funded and over-burdened. States continue to make, and change, decisions about Medicaid that, among other things, will affect the amount of long-term care assistance available in each state, the eligibility criteria and number of persons eligible for that assistance, and the types of services that will be reimbursed.

The Deficit Reduction Act of 2005

President George W. Bush signed The Deficit Reduction Omnibus Reconciliation Act of 2005 on February 8, 2006. The new law tightens Medicaid's long-term care eligibility rules and allows for the nationwide expansion of the Long-Term Care (LTC) Partnership program.

This is great news for the long-term care insurance industry as it will encourage proper planning for future long-term care needs, and allow for the sale of Qualified State Long-Term Care Insurance policies (QSLTCI) under the new partnership program.

Changes to Medicaid Eligibility

The changes to Medicaid eligibility will make it harder for individuals to qualify for coverage. Such changes include:

* Extension of look-back period for the transfer of assets from three years to five years prior to applying for Medicaid coverage. Note on grandfathering: The five-year look-back period will be phased in, as it will only affect transfers made after the law's effective date.

* Applicants will need to meet the required spend-down limits prior to the start of their penalty period (if they have a penalty period).

* Legislation will deny Medicaid coverage for nursing-home care to any applicant with home equity valued above $500,000 (up to $750,000 in some states).

Expansion of Partnership Long-Term Care Insurance Policies

The new law also includes the national expansion and availability of LTCI Partnership plans. Each individual state will have the opportunity to implement a Partnership program. Partnership policies help to protect state Medicaid budgets by requiring that the benefits of those qualifying insurance policies be paid before Medicaid benefits can be accessed. (The four existing partnership programs in CA, CT, IN, and NY will be grandfathered.)

The new Partnership policies allow consumers to protect a portion of their assets that they would typically need to spend down prior to qualifying for Medicaid coverage—ensuring that more of the funds accumulated for retirement will be protected.

Under the expansion of state Partnerships, states must have the same requirements for Partnership and Non-Partnership policies. The objective, as states elect to participate, is to have uniform requirements. Essentially, any tax-qualified LTCI policy approved by a state insurance department that meets the requirements of the federal Partnership program would qualify for asset protection, on a dollar-for-dollar basis, up to the policy maximum.

Assets that must be spent down in order to qualify for Medicaid include:

* cash
* checking/saving accounts
* CDs
* savings bonds
* investment accounts/mutual funds/stocks
* IRA's and other retirement accounts
* vacation homes and investment properties

- second car
- certain real estate or personal property not in use

Assets that a person can keep for purposes of qualifying for Medicaid include:

- a home (a principal residence with equity under $500,000)
- household goods
- personal effects
- automobile—one per household
- life insurance (no more than $1500 in cash surrender value)
- irrevocable prepaid burial plan.
- property essential to the individual's self support (perhaps a small business)
- income producing property—other than cash, with some restrictions (like farmed land)

Reverse Mortgages and Medicaid

Reverse mortgages do not affect Medicare (including Medicare Part D) or Social Security income. However, the proceeds from a reverse mortgage CAN affect local income-based programs in your area, and the big one—Medicaid.

The first thing to remember is that aging adults should answer a lot of questions regarding their plans for the cash flow or lump sum received from a reverse mortgage:

- Are they already in poor health?
- Do they intend to "gift" the money away to relatives?
- Are they using the money to pay for in-home care?
- Do they have long-term care insurance already?
- Are they planning on applying for Medicaid anytime soon?

If the answer to any of these questions is **yes**, they would be well advised to consult a local elder law attorney (*www.naela.org*). Keep in mind that most elder law attorneys need education about reverse mortgages. It is always a good idea to check with an elder law attorney who understands all aspects of Reverse Mortgages and Medicaid. An aging adult may also be wise to consider having a son, daughter or other advocate accompany them when consulting an attorney.

The bottom line is that if someone needs to be on Medicaid soon, or already there, then "gifting" and additional cash flow in their checking accounts or savings accounts can knock them out of eligibility quickly!

If your family member is thinking about taking the "lump sum" option available through a reverse mortgage, you might ask them to consider leaving the money in the line of credit. When they make a withdrawal from the line of credit (to pay bills, buy a new appliance, fix the air conditioner or heater) they must spend that money the same month that the withdrawal from the line of credit hits their checking account. Even then, they need to keep receipts for service and goods purchased to prove that they didn't give the money away.

If that extra cash flow sits in their checking or savings account for more than 30 days, it could knock them out of eligibility.

If a senior decides that they want to receive the monthly check to increase their cash flow, they should make sure that they need the money every month to pay bills. If that checking account starts adding up, or if they are above the allowed amount of income because of the additional cash flow, they may be getting into trouble.

Do not assume that your family member knows the rules, because the rules are complicated and change regularly. Talk to someone who knows and studies these laws all of the time.

Prenuptial Agreements

For second marriages, this information is particularly important.

"What's mine is mine, what's his is his. They won't touch MY money for HIS long-term care, right?"

Yes, they will. Prenuptial agreements hold no weight when it comes to Medicaid. When two people are married, their assets become marital property. So even if Nancy has $1 million dollars, and Robert has $5,000 dollars, it does not really matter. If one of them needs care, and they have no long-term care insurance, they will have to go through the spend-down process considering both of their combined assets.

Mandatory Estate Recovery

With the changes in federal law enacted in August 1993, the state must seek recovery of Medicaid expenditures from the estate of a deceased individual who was 55 or older when he or she received assistance.

This means that when the person on Medicaid dies, the state will collect the amount they spent on that person's care from the remaining estate. The state must include all real estate, personal property, and other assets included within an estate under the state's probate law. The state may also include other property in which the individual had an interest at the time of death. If the deceased Medicaid recipient has a spouse still living in the home (community spouse), that spouse can usually continue living in the home until his or her death, before the state will seek recovery. A Medicaid lien is usually placed on the property of the Medicaid recipient.

Transferring Assets

"I'll Just Give It All Away!"

When a person applies for Medicaid to pay for medical care, federal law requires the state to consider recent transfers of assets and monetary gifts. If a person or his or her spouse has transferred assets for less than fair market value in the 60 months (5 years) prior to applying for Medicaid, or at any time after applying, the applicant will be considered "ineligible" for a period of time based on the amount transferred. In the case of assets transferred to a "trust," the look-back period is the same; 60 months. The look-back period means that the state can go back 5 years and see if any transfers have been made and add them (based on a specific calculation) to the ineligibility period.

Divorce

If Robert and Nancy had given $120,000 to their wonderful daughter Susan, for safe keeping 6 years prior to Robert's stroke, Robert would almost immediately be eligible for Medicaid.

But what if Susan's husband, Scott, decided that he wanted a divorce? Technically, in most states that money would be considered marital property and would be divided in half, leaving Susan with only $60,000 of her parent's money.

Lawsuits

Susan has her parent's $120,000 in a bank account in her and her husband's names. Husband Scott is in a car accident, and the other party sues Scott for damages beyond what his insurance company will pay. The plaintiff's lawyer sees $120,000 sitting in their account. If he wins the case, they may lose it all.

Financial Aid

Susan and Scott have a daughter who will be 18 in a few months and is looking forward to going away to college. The family applies for financial aid, but because they have Susan's parent's $120,000 in their account, their daughter does not qualify for financial aid.

Buying Toys

Susan and Scott have always been fairly responsible, but have decided that they need that new boat. Susan's parents, Robert and Nancy, will not know if they borrow just $20,000. The kids will be sure to pay it back…eventually.

Comprehensive Long-Term Care Solutions Using Private Pay Strategies

CHAPTER SEVEN

Traditional Long-Term Care Insurance and the Partnership Plan

How Much Does Long-Term Care Insurance Cost?

O f course, the cost of long-term care insurance depends on many different choices and options. The more bells and whistles, the more costly the plan. The most important thing to remember is that long-term care insurance premiums will NEVER cost as much as a few months in a nursing home without the insurance (see Chapter 1). The problem for most people is that long-term care insurance premiums may seem unaffordable, even though they are the most cost effective way to plan ahead.

Recognizing this, the federal government introduced the LTC Partnership Program.

The Partnership Program couples the purchase of long-term care insurance with eligibility for Medicaid coverage for LTC services. With the purchase of a Partnership policy, a consumer can become eligible for Medicaid coverage after using the insurance benefits without having to exhaust his or her own assets to qualify for such coverage. Assets equal to the amount expended by the insurance policy are not considered countable assets for purposes of Medicaid eligibility and are exempt from the Medicaid estate recovery provisions. (One significant caveat; those with home equity exceeding $500,000 are not eligible for Medicaid even with the Partnership policy, although states may increase that ceiling to $750,000.)

Traditional Long-Term Care Insurance

Traditional long-term care insurance used to be viewed as "nursing-home insurance" because most policies from 15 years ago only offered that one option. Today that is hardly the case; long-term care insurance now covers adult day care, in-home care, assisted living, and nursing-home care. These policies are considered comprehensive in nature. Now we refer to long-term care insurance as "lifestyle insurance."

Who Cannot Get Long-Term Care Insurance?

Underwriting Explained

When you apply for a long-term care insurance plan, you must go through underwriting. Underwriting means that the company will check your medical records to determine what medical problems you may currently have, or have had in the past. They want to know your overall health history. If you have been diagnosed with short-term memory loss, Alzheimer's disease, Parkinson's disease, Multiple Sclerosis, Lou Gehrig's disease, or if you have had a stroke with permanent physical impairment, you may not qualify. People who have survived cancer and are treatment free for a certain length of time can often qualify. Each insurance company has their own underwriting guidelines. It is best to talk to your agent or call the company directly with any specific questions about health issues. Height and weight are also a consideration when applying. Sometimes the insurance company will send a registered nurse to the home to ask a few questions and take some more medical history, or they may just call on the phone for a brief interview.

Qualifying to USE the Benefits of a Long-Term Care Insurance Plan

Activities of Daily Living

When it is time to use your tax-qualified long-term care insurance plan (taxes to be discussed in a later chapter), the insured person must need help or substantial assistance with 2 out of 6 activities of daily living for a period of 90 days or greater. This need for care must be certified by a licensed healthcare practitioner such as a nurse or physician.

These activities of daily living include:

- bathing
- dressing
- eating
- toileting
- continence
- transferring (i.e. moving from the bed to a chair)

Or the insured must have a cognitive impairment like Alzheimer's disease or dementia. A cognitive impairment means that although a person may be physically able to perform all of the activities listed above, they cannot remember or rationalize how to do those activities. One example would be bathing; sometimes people with dementia are physically able to take a bath, but cannot remember to do so, cannot remember why this is important, or perhaps when getting dressed, they put on 5 shirts instead of one.

Comprehensive vs. Facility-Only Plans

Comprehensive Plans

A comprehensive plan covers all aspects of long-term care: in-home care, adult day care, assisted living, and nursing-home care. These plans are designed to help people stay at home longer and also to assist them with transitions to other levels of care as needed. Most consumers want to stay at home for as long as possible. A comprehensive plan will satisfy that desire.

Facility-Only Coverage

Facility-only plans are still available on the market today. Facility-only plans pay for just that, facility care only. Usually this includes assisted living and nursing-home care. A facility only plan makes the most sense for folks who do not have a large network of family and friends around them, and for people who know that this may be their only option in the future. Facility-only plans are less costly than comprehensive plans but again, offer payment only for nursing-home and assisted-living care. The insured person cannot live at home and use the benefits of a facility-only plan.

Benefit Period

The benefit period is the length of time during which the policy will actually pay for care. There are many different benefit periods available including 2 years, 3 years, 4 years, 5 years, 7 years, 10 years, and unlimited lifetime coverage. When purchasing long-term care insurance, keep in mind that premiums are paid for potentially the next 20 years (or until the policy holder needs care), but the plan will only last about as long as the benefit period originally selected.

People often ask, "How do I know which benefit period to choose?" "How do I know how long I might need care?"

Obviously there is no way to really determine how long a person might need care. However, the best advice for each individual is to take a look at their own personal health history and their family history; if there is a history of chronic disease such as Alzheimer's, Parkinson's, MS, or Lou Gehrig's disease, it might be worthwhile to consider a longer benefit period.

The average length of stay in a nursing home is about 2.8 years; the average care-giving time at home is about 4.1 years.

Daily Benefit Amount

The daily benefit amount is the maximum amount a plan will pay on a daily or weekly basis. Some policies now pay based on a weekly or monthly maximum. In this case, it is important to know the average cost of care in the local area. In the Midwest, for example, the average cost of care for a semi-private nursing home bed is about $165 per day. Therefore, the plan should pay a maximum of $4,950 per month. In New York, the current cost of a semi-private nursing home bed is around $340 per day or $10,200 per month. Consider the cost of care in the area where you live and the cost of care in an area where you might retire, and plan accordingly.

A semi-private room in a nursing home means that two people share a room. A private room in a nursing home means that the room is for one person only. A private room will cost significantly more than a semi-private room. Be sure to factor in the extra cost if a private room is expected.

For some people the insurance policy's daily benefit amount does not need to cover the entire cost of care. If there is some Social Security income or pension income that can pick up a portion of the long-term care costs, then perhaps some premium can be saved by having a lower daily benefit amount. Keep in mind however, that $135/day covers the cost of room and board only in the Midwest, not the added cost of prescription drugs, supplies such as adult incontinence protection, and other necessities. The additional expense of these items can add as much as 20% per day on to the cost of a nursing home bed.

Elimination Period

The elimination period is similar to a deductible or a waiting period. This is the length of time a person must wait before their plan will begin to pay. Elimination periods vary from company to company and plan to plan. The elimination period choices include 0 days, 30 days, 60 days, 90 days, 100 days, and 180 days. Some plans will offer to waive the elimination period for home care under certain circumstances, and some offer riders that will eliminate or decrease waiting periods. Be aware that some elimination periods are based on dates of service. Therefore, if only one day of home care is needed per week and the elimination period is 30 days, it could take as much as 30 weeks to satisfy that elimination period. On the other hand, many companies today will allow one day of home care to count as 7 days toward the elimination period. This is a nice strategy and is useful in encouraging people to stay home longer.

The shorter the elimination period, the more expensive the premium.

Inflation Protection Options

The average cost of health care rises anywhere from 4%-7% per year. Therefore $135 per day today won't be enough coverage 10 years from now when the cost is actually around

$250 per day, so it is important to build in some protection against the cost of inflation.

There are typically three types of inflation protection that are available. One is compound inflation protection, which provides an automatic increase in benefits every year (usually at 5%) with no corresponding increase in premium. This is the most expensive inflation protection, but is well worth the investment. For consumers who buy long-term care insurance at younger ages, for example anyone under age 70, compound inflation protection offers the most complete coverage.

Simple inflation protection is also usually at 5% per year but is not compounded. This inflation protection will grow at a slower rate than compound inflation protection and is often recommended for folks over age 70. There is no corresponding increase in premium.

Finally, there is a future purchase option offered on some plans. This option allows the consumer to decide at a later time whether they would like to buy a greater daily benefit amount to catch up with the current cost of care. If no extra benefit is purchased, the daily benefit amount remains the same and the premium does not increase. If extra benefit is purchased, the premium increases to the new benefit level. No further underwriting is required for future purchase option benefit increases.

Care Coordination Benefits

Some plans will offer care coordination as a built-in benefit. Care coordination is a valuable service for both the person receiving care and for the other family members involved. Long-term care insurers recognize that sometimes it is difficult for a senior or a family member to know which services in their local area might be most appropriate and give the best quality care available. Care coordinators are licensed professionals such as Registered Nurses and Licensed Social Workers who have experience in home health and coordinating care for seniors in their local areas. Some companies will require the plan member to use a care coordinator designated by the insurer. Other companies will allow a family to choose that care coordinator. They will allot a certain amount of money to be used toward a comprehensive in-home evaluation and plan of care. Either way, this service is invaluable and takes the fear and confusion out of selecting a long-term care provider. Care coordinators are not "gatekeepers"; they are simply healthcare professionals who know the system and the local resources. They are there for guidance and assistance along the way.

Home Care and Community Care Benefits

Home and Community Care includes services provided by a licensed home health agency. This can include services from a Registered Nurse, Licensed Practical Nurse, Physical Therapist, Occupational Therapist, Nurse's Aide, homemaker services (non-medical services), at-home hospice care, and adult day care. Some plans with enhanced home care provisions, or riders, will also allow (with authorization) a friend or family member to provide care. That family member will be reimbursed for their time and expense. A family member usually cannot be someone who normally lives in the same home as the person going on claim. In other words, most long-term care insurance companies do not want to pay a spouse to be the sole caregiver.

Facility Care

Facility care most often refers to care received in a nursing home, hospice facility, or assisted-living facility. The plan will usually cover room and board, nursing care, maintenance or personal care, and hospice care in that facility. Most plans will also offer a bed reservation benefit, meaning that if a person leaves the facility for the weekend, or is hospitalized, the insurer will pay for that amount of time to hold the bed even though the insured is not in the facility. Most bed reservation benefits last about 30 days per policy year.

Respite Care Benefits

Respite care, simply defined, is a break for the caregiver. For example, if daughter Susan is caring for her father, she may need a break from time to time. If she decides to take a long weekend and go on vacation, a formal caregiver can be hired to take her place. Respite care can be received in a nursing home or adult day care, in-home, or in a hospice facility. The insurer will pay the maximum daily benefit for up to 21 days per year on average. The insured does not have to meet the elimination period in order to use respite care benefits.

Alternate Plan of Care

"Alternate plan of care" usually refers to services that are not already clearly defined in the plan. Most alternate plans of care must be approved by the insurer, but would include services designed to enhance quality of life or designed to keep a person safe in their home for a longer period of time. Examples include a personal emergency service, like LifeLine, or perhaps a wheelchair ramp that would enhance accessibility to the insured's home.

Caregiver Training

Caregiver training is useful when an informal caregiver needs to learn how to bathe, transfer, feed, or dress someone receiving long-term care. A licensed or formally trained professional will provide the training to the informal caregiver. This ensures that the care being received is quality care, and is provided in a safe and efficient manner. This training will be paid for by the plan.

Bells and Whistles (The Riders)

Riders can be purchased in addition to the standard long-term care insurance plan and offer flexibility in plan design.

Shared Benefits

Some plans will allow spouses and families to share benefits. One example would be the sharing of a benefit between husband and wife. In this case, the husband and wife choose an 8-year plan. If he needs to use 6 years of the plan, she will have 2 years left to use when she needs long-term care. A shared benefit plan might be recommended to a couple who have been married for many years and who are roughly the same age.

Survivorship

Survivorship typically means that if both spouses are insured by the same company with no claim having been made in 7-10 years, and one spouse passes away, the other spouse's plan will be paid up in full. There will be no further premium due for the surviving spouse and coverage will continue.

Return of Premium

Return of premium takes away the fear: "If I don't use it, I'll lose it!" This simply means that if a claim has never been made and the insured person passes away, the premium paid will be returned to the surviving heirs. There are several variations on the theme and each company handles return of premium differently. Pay close attention to contract language in the policy.

Waiver of Premium

In many cases, waiver of premium is a built-in feature of a long-term care insurance plan, but in some cases it can be purchased as an extra rider. Waiver of premium means that when the insured files a claim and begins using their benefits, they no longer pay premiums to the insurance company. Usually, waiver of premium goes into effect after the elimination period has been satisfied.

Indemnity

The typical long-term care insurance plan is a reimbursement plan, meaning that the insurance company reimburses the care providers after a claim has been submitted. However, some plans now offer an indemnity situation. This type of plan will pay the insured the daily or monthly benefit, and it is up to the insured to pay the care providers. This type of plan is more flexible and usually more expensive. However, the insured has more options when choosing a care provider. For instance, instead of using a local home health agency, the insured person may want to pay a son or daughter to care for them. Indemnity plans require that the insured, or their legal representative, makes good choices about care and is able to use the money wisely.

Important Consideration When Choosing a Long-Term Care Plan

Ratings

The financial ratings of a company are important when considering purchasing a long-term care insurance plan. The recommendation is to choose a company with an AM BEST rating of A + or better.

Assets

Assets of the insurance company should be in the BILLIONS.

Discounts

Some long-term care insurers will allow for group discounts through employers, or "affinity" group discounts through a local organization. Senior clubs and organizations all across America offer discounts from 5%-10% on long-term care insurance. Not all companies permit these types of discounts, however there are some discounts that almost all long-term care insurers include in their plans. Those include spousal (or partner) discounts and good health discounts. Spousal discounts are applied when a couple applies for the insurance together. Discounts of this kind range anywhere from 30-50%. Good health discounts are given when the applicant is in excellent health. Each company has its own underwriting guidelines for health discounts. These will range from 10%-15%.

Tax Considerations

Currently, there are some tax advantages regarding tax qualified long-term care insurance plans. At the federal level, premiums for long-term care insurance fall into the "medical expense" category, so if the premium (or the premium plus other medical expenses) is over 7.5% of the adjusted gross income, part of that premium is tax deductible. Taxpayers must be able to itemize in order to take advantage of the federal deduction. It is important to talk to a tax advisor or accountant for that information, as it changes every year.

Business owners, especially those with C-Corporations, can deduct the full cost of long-term care insurance protection for themselves and designated individuals, including spouses.

On the state level, 26 states offer some form of deduction or tax credit for long-term care insurance premiums. In the state of Missouri, for example, premiums are 100% tax deductible.

This is an "above the line" deduction so there is no need to itemize to take advantage of the savings. In Kentucky the premium is 100% tax deductible. Again, it is important to see an accountant or tax advisor for tax advantages state by state.

Tax Qualified Plans vs. Non-Tax Qualified Plans

To make matters a little more complicated, there are two types of standard long-term care insurance plans available. Tax qualified plans follow the federal HIPAA law (Health Insurance Portability and Accountability Act). For these plans, the insured must need assistance with 2 out of 6 activities of daily living, for a period of 90 days or greater, in order to qualify to use their benefits. This law protects consumers in several ways. It insures that long-term care insurance is truly designed for long-term care… greater than 90 days. The benefits received are not considered taxable income. Tax qualified plans are guaranteed renewable. This means that your coverage can never be cancelled, as long as you pay your premiums.

Non-tax qualified plans allow the consumer to access benefits more quickly. With these plans, the insured only needs to prove that they require assistance with 1 out of 5 activities of daily living, with an attending physician's statement. Non-tax qualified plans are usually a bit more expensive than tax qualified plans. The jury is still out on whether or not the benefits are taxable as income. In the insurance world, there is a great debate on the pros and cons of each plan. Sticking with a tax-qualified plan is currently my recommendation.

Payment Options for Long-Term Care Insurance

Annual Premium Payment

"Annual premium payment" means that the insured person will pay premiums yearly for a lifetime or until they use their long-term care insurance. Payments can also be made monthly, quarterly, or semi-annually. Like auto or homeowners insurance, if payments are made on a monthly, quarterly, or semi-annual basis, there is usually an additional fee. Once the insured has a claim approved, most policies will waive the premium after the elimination period has been satisfied.

10-Pay

The 10-pay option allows the insured to pay a higher premium for a shorter period of time—10 years. After 10 years of premium payment, no further premiums are due.

Pay to 65

Some plans offer the option for the insured person to pay premiums until they are 65. At age 65, no further premium is due. This is a nice option because at retirement age, income may be significantly less than that of working-age adults.

Lump-Sum (One-Time) Payment

Some consumers have the option to pay a one-time, lump-sum premium. This means that no further premium is ever due. Many business owners find this option attractive for the tax deduction in the year that they purchase the policy. Asset-based, long-term care insurance is also a one-time payment.

CHAPTER EIGHT

Annuity-Based Long-Term Care and the The Pension Protection Act of 2006

O n August 17, 2006, the President signed into law The Pension Protection Act of 2006 (the "Act"). Individuals owning annuity contracts can now have long-term care riders with special tax advantages. The Act allows the cash value of annuity contracts to be used to pay premiums on long-term care contracts. The payment of premiums in this manner will reduce the cost basis of the annuity contract. In addition, the Act allows annuity contracts without long-term care riders to be exchanged for contracts with such a rider in a tax-free transfer under Section 1035 of the Internal Revenue Code of 1986, as amended ("IRC"). This provision may prove beneficial to individuals who own annuities with a low cost basis and those who are not in the best of health. The cash value of the annuity can be used to purchase long-term care insurance. This provision is effective for exchanges which take place after 2009.

An example of how an annuity-based long-term care plan could help someone is illustrated in Exhibit 8.1. For this example, we will call our client Bob, age 70, and recently widowed. His children lived out of town and they were very concerned about what would happen if dad needed some additional care in the future. Since Bob had some health concerns and was recently diagnosed with diabetes, along with a history of heart disease, he was not a good candidate for traditional long-term care insurance. However, by taking advantage of an annuity based long-term care strategy that takes advantage of the Pension Protection Act, Bob could likely be insured. By taking his $140,000 fixed annuity with a cost basis of only 40,000 (i.e. the amount he actually deposited) and using the IRS 1035 tax-free exchange from his existing fixed annuity to a new annuity that complied with the rules laid out in the Pension Protection Act, Bob's $140,000 fixed annuity could continue to earn interest. However, if he needed long-term care to pay for home care, assisted living, or skilled care he now had a long-term care pool of money equal to $420,000. (See exhibit 8.1.)*

* Not all products are available in all states.

Exhibit 8.1

Bob (70)

Current Situation

$300,000 Money Market

$37,000 Checking

$140,000 Fixed Annuity *(Cost Basis 40,000)*

$240,000 Home

* recently widowed
* adult children live out of town
* health concerns — insulin diabetes with history of heart disease

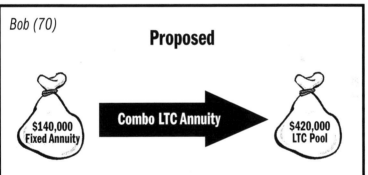

Bob (70)

Proposed

$140,000 Fixed Annuity

Combo LTC Annuity

$420,000 LTC Pool

Hypothetically, by repositioning his fixed annuity...

* Bob retains his $140,000 in cash value plus an additional $280,000 for a total of $420,000 for long-term care.
* His benefits may be used for home care, assisted living, and skilled care.
* He pays no annual premiums.
* As his annuity grows, so does his LTC!
  (Assuming he does not use his LTC benefit.)

CHAPTER NINE

Life Insurance/ Long-Term Care Strategy

Until recently, the thought of using a life insurance policy to pay for long-term care expenses was unthinkable. However, with the first baby boomers reaching the milestone of age 65 on January 1 of 2011, the insurance companies have begun offering long-term care coverage as a rider on term life policies as well as whole life and universal life policies.

The basic concept is that the insurance company will allow the insured to accelerate the death benefit of the policy if the insured is unable to perform two of the six activities of daily living (eating, dressing, bathing, transferring, toileting or continence) or if the insured is cognitively impaired. The most attractive feature of this type of plan is the ability of the insured to use the money to pay for home healthcare, assisted-living, or skilled care. The policy will even allow you to pick who your caregiver is—including family members. This strategy is illustrated in Exhibit 9.1.

Exhibit 9.1

Sue (45)

Current Situation

- Sue is a single mom and has children going to college.
- She currently has a 20-year term and is in year 18.
- Sue feels strongly about never wanting to go to a nursing home.
- She would like to buy long-term care insurance, but does not feel like she can afford the premiums.

Sue (45)

Proposed

Sue's Solution—30 Year Term with LTC Rider*

- provide for an LTC Program by replacing existing term insurance
- choice of where she wants to receive her care
- choice of caregiver (even family members)
- provide tax-free death benefit to her children if she does not need long-term care—$500,000

* Not all products are available in all states.

CHAPTER TEN

Asset-Based Long-Term Care Strategy

"Legacy assets" are those assets in a retiree's portfolio that do not support their lifestyle, but are available in case of some serious emergency (rainy day money!). These assets, if (hopefully) never needed, will probably pass to the clients' children, church, or charity after they die. The one most significant risk to those assets is the need to pay for long-term care.

Many people in this situation resist the idea of conventional long-term care insurance, not wanting to admit that they might need it, and taking the position that they can pay for any care out of pocket. They are choosing to "self insure." For these individuals, the ideal planning approach would be to "invest" some of their legacy assets in such a way that the assets can be worth as much as possible whenever they may be needed to pay for care…in the home, assisted-living facility, or nursing home. If not needed, the money would then pass to the intended heirs, with no "use it, or lose it" issues as with conventional long-term care insurance.

To employ this strategy, money is transferred from its current location (bank account, fixed annuity, etc.) into a specially-designed life insurance policy with riders that prepay the death benefit, and additionally to reimburse the insured for the incurred costs of long-term care. Depending on age, sex and health status, the money paid into one of these policies may be worth twice as much if the insured dies without ever needing to use it. Also, if needed for convalescent care, the insured can receive up to five times the amount of money deposited into the contract. Any money not used for that purpose would then pass to the heirs at death (See Exhibit 10.1).*

While invested in the insurance policy, the client's money is safe and available for any other reason at any time. There is usually a money-back guarantee that assures that the policy-holder will always have access to the funds. Rather than a typical "purchase" of insurance, the transaction is more like "moving money from one account to another"…a cash value account that provides the same "savings" features as the bank, bond, or annuity from which it came.

Because the actual cost of long-term care is so great (potentially $70,000 per year or more) and the average need exceeds 2 years, these policies are usually purchased with a rider that extends the long-term care benefits after the death benefit has been exhausted. These riders effectively double or triple the benefit so that in the example (See Exhibit 10.1), a $50,000 premium deposit can provide as much as $250,000 in total long-term care benefits, providing as much as six years worth of protection.

This approach is ideal for those individuals who reject the idea of purchasing conventional, annual-premium long-term care insurance policies and take the position that if they ever need long-term convalescent care, they will pay for it using their own assets.

* Not all products are available in all states.

Exhibit 10.1

Mary's Hypothetical Situation

Proposed Strategy

- It provides LTC by repositioning assets.
- Mary can choose where to receive care with income tax-free LTC benefits.
- Income tax-free death benefit for children if she does not need long-term care.
- 100% of the premium is returned (within the time-frame and conditions allowed in the policy) if Mary changes her mind or finds a better solution.
- LTC benefits are guaranteed without worries of future premium increases.

Note: The death benefit on these policies typically declines dollar for dollar based on the amount of LTC benefit needed. If Mary needs a $20,000 LTC withdrawal, her death benefit would be reduced by $20,000 to $80,000.

Mary (65)

Proposed
Asset-Preservation Strategy
Combo Life & LTC

(65-year-old female non-smoker in good health)

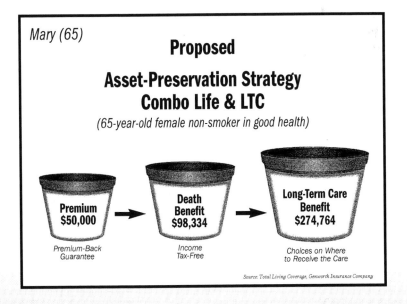

Premium $50,000	Death Benefit $98,334	Long-Term Care Benefit $274,764
Premium-Back Guarantee	Income Tax-Free	Choices on Where to Receive the Care

Source: Total Living Coverage, Genworth Insurance Company

For individuals who do not, for whatever reason, want to own any life insurance, there is an alternative. Since the objective is to leverage up the individual's assets if long-term care is needed, some insurance companies are now offering fixed index annuities with guaranteed income riders that double should the individual enter a nursing home (See Exhibit 10.2).

Finally, of all the contingencies faced in retirement, long-term care is probably the most difficult and perhaps the most costly...financially as well as emotionally. These asset-based long-term care strategies allow wise consumers to manage their money, and to provide significantly for such a possibility without committing large annual insurance premiums to something they sincerely hope will never be needed. Since the money to do this must reside somewhere, these asset-based long-term care products provide a safe and financially rewarding option.

Exhibit 10.2

Income Preferred Series Calculator

Year Issue	Attained Age	Income Base	Withdrawal Percentage	Withdrawal Payment	Enhanced Withdrawal Payment
0	75	$354,000	n/a	n/a	n/a
1	76	$354,000	5.90%	$20,886	n/a
2	77	$354,000	6.00%	$21,240	n/a
3	78	$362,385	6.00%	$21,743	$43,486
4	79	$385,940	6.00%	$23,156	$46,313
5	80	$411,026	6.00%	$24,662	$49,323
6	81	$437,743	6.00%	$26,265	$52,529
7	82	$466,196	6.00%	$27,972	$55,944
8	83	$496,499	6.00%	$29,790	$59,580
9	84	$528,771	6.00%	$31,726	$63,453
10	85	$563,141	6.00%	$33,788	$67,577
11	86	$599,745	6.00%	$35,985	$71,969
12	87	$638,729	6.00%	$38,324	$76,647
13	88	$680,246	6.00%	$40,815	$81,630
14	89	$724,462	6.00%	$43,468	$86,935
15	90	$771,552	6.00%	$46,293	$92,586
16	91	$821,703	6.00%	$49,302	$98,604
17	92	$875,114	6.00%	$52,507	$105,014
18	93	$931,996	6.00%	$55,920	$111,840
19	94	$992,576	6.00%	$59,555	$119,109
20	95	$1,057,094	6.00%	$63,426	$126,851

* Not all products are available in all states.

Product:
Fixed Index Annuity*

Initial Premium:
$300,000 (includes any applicable bonus)

Issue Age: 75

Years to Defer: 10

Withdrawal Attained Age: 85

Joint Annuitant: No

Mode of Withdrawal: Annual

The printouts and results displayed by this calculator are approved for consumer use. Please note the actual use and inputting of values are only for appointed LTC producers. The assumptions used in this illustration are guaranteed based on the assumptions you provide in the calculation. The use of alternative premium, age, product, deferral years, and joint life assumptions may produce significantly different results.

CHAPTER ELEVEN

Long-Term Care Strategy Using IRA Money

While most people use their IRA to supplement retirement, many times waiting until age 70 $^1/_2$, at which point the mandatory required minimum distribution rules apply, some people have chosen to take a portion of their IRA and fund an IRA-based annuity which then systematically funds a 20 pay life insurance plan with long-term care features. This type of IRA-based long-term care policy is unique in the sense that it starts out as an IRA annuity policy, also known as a tax qualified annuity, and then over a twenty year period makes equal distribution internally to the insurance carrier and funds the life insurance. The owner of the IRA annuity will receive annually for 20 years a 1099-R (the IRS tax form that reports the taxable amount of an IRA distribution) on the amount of the IRA that is moved annually to fund the life insurance policy. Let's look at an example. We will use Tim, age 60, recently widowed, and retired. While he feels very secure about his retirement income, his main concern is long-term care and how to pay for it. Like many people his age he is what we call "qualified money rich … non-qual-

Exhibit 11.1

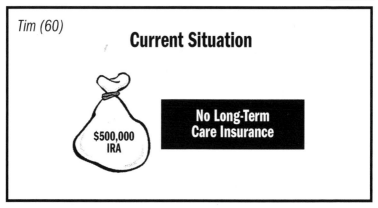

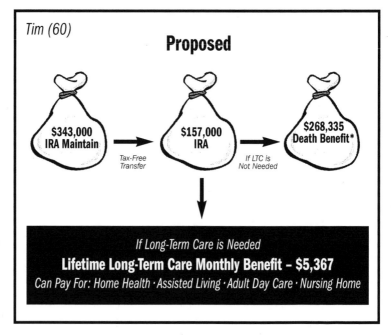

* Not all products are available in all states.

ified poor." In other words, Tim has a lot more IRA type money (before tax) than he does after tax money. By taking advantage of a tax-free trustee to trustee transfer, Tim is able to reposition $157,000 of his $500,000 IRA account into an IRA-based annuity which will fund a life policy which in turn will provide a pool of long term money should he need it in the future. By doing this, he will create a death benefit in the amount of $268,335 that will be paid to his children upon his death. More importantly than the death benefit is that should Tim ever need long-term care, this policy will provide a monthly benefit of $5,367 that can be used to pay for home healthcare, assisted living, adult day care or even skilled nursing-home care (See Exhibit 11.1).

Let's look at another example. This example will show the impact of using an IRA-based long-term policy for a married couple. Both Beth, age 60, and her husband Bob, age 65, are concerned about long-term care but up to this point have been scared away from purchasing traditional stand-alone long-term care policies due to the requirement that annual premiums have to be paid. While they do not need additional income from Bob's IRA, they would like to help their children avoid paying taxes on the IRA account when both Bob and Beth have passed away. In the case of a married couple, this is when the taxes on an IRA are due. By taking advantage of a tax-free, trustee to trustee transfer, Bob decides to transfer $240,000 from his IRA into an IRA annuity that will fund a 20 year pay life insurance policy. Bob will receive a 1099-R annually for the IRA dollar amount that is internally moved from his IRA annuity to the life insurance policy. Beth is included, along with Bob as an insured on the life policy so

Exhibit 11.2

Beth (60) Bob (65)

Long-Term Care Strategy for Couples Using IRA

**$540,000
IRA**   **$145,000
Checking/
Savings**   **$3,800/mo
Pension/
Social Security**

- They are concerned about long-term care.
- They have been scared away from traditional LTC insurance premiums.
- They would like to avoid taxes on IRA at 2nd death.

Beth (60) Bob (65)

Beth and Bob's Solution

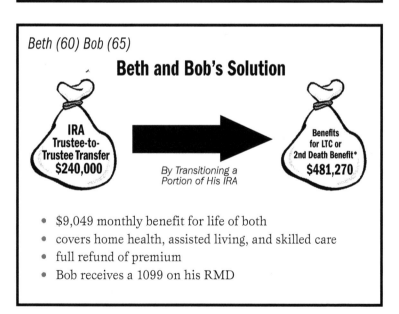

**IRA
Trustee-to-
Trustee Transfer
$240,000**

*By Transitioning a
Portion of His IRA*

**Benefits
for LTC or
2nd Death Benefit***
$481,270

- $9,049 monthly benefit for life of both
- covers home health, assisted living, and skilled care
- full refund of premium
- Bob receives a 1099 on his RMD

* Not all products are available in all states.

that upon the death of Bob and Beth, their children will receive an initial death benefit in the amount of $459,164. The life insurance portion of this program is referred to as a second-to-die life insurance policy. More importantly, by making this IRA transfer they have secured $9,049 of monthly long-term care benefit for both of them! This monthly long-term care benefit can be used to pay for home healthcare, assisted living, adult day care, or even skilled nursing care. In addition to the above benefits, should they ever need to withdraw their $240,000, this type of policy offers a full refund of premium (See Exhibit 11.2).

Long-Term Care Solutions Using Goverment Benefits/Legal Strategies

CHAPTER TWELVE

Legal Documents Needed for Long-Term Care Planning

Legal Matters

One of the most important things to set in motion is the legal paperwork! A durable power of attorney for health care and a financial power of attorney are essential, along with an advanced directive or living will.

Elder law attorneys can help with:

- trusts
- wills
- durable powers of attorney
- Medicaid and VA benefits
- advanced medical directives
- other important legal issues and documents

What is a "Power of Attorney"?

A power of attorney (POA) is a document whereby one person (called the "principal") authorizes another individual or entity (called an "agent" or "attorney-in-fact") to act on behalf of the principal. The most common uses for a POA are financial transactions and health care decisions. Most states have one set of laws governing financial POAs and a second set of laws governing POAs for health care decisions. Therefore, it is the common and recommended practice not to mix the two purposes into one document. An individual desiring to have a POA covering both financial and medical situations should prepare two separate POAs, one dealing with financial issues and the second dealing with medical issues.

When Should I Have a Financial Power of Attorney?

Persons with physical handicaps or limitations often set up financial POAs, with a family member as the agent, to allow the family member to do such routine matters as making withdrawals from the principal's bank account. It would otherwise be a burden for the principal with physical limitations to make the short trips personally to perform the banking transactions.

The second reason for preparation of a financial POA is preventative in nature. If you lose the mental capacity to handle your own financial affairs, without a durable power of attorney (see below), your family members will need to go to court and have a guardian or conservator appointed over your assets. If you have previously set up a durable power of attorney and then lose mental capacity, the agent named in your POA will be able to handle your financial affairs without the time and attorney fees necessary for going to the court to get a guardian and conservator appointed.

A *"durable"* POA is one that remains in force even after the principal (i.e. the individual who executed the POA) loses mental capacity. Unless a POA is "durable," it will become ineffective at the time the principal becomes incompetent. Thus, a POA which is not "durable" fails to protect you against the potential of your family having to go to court and get a guardian and conservator appointed over your assets.

What Makes a Power of Attorney "Durable"?

This is a matter of state law. The Uniform Durable Power of Attorney Act has been adopted by 48 states and provides the following definition:

> "A durable power of attorney is a power of attorney by which a principal, in writing, designates another as his attorney in fact and the writing contains the words, 'This power of attorney shall not be affected by subsequent disability or incapacity of the principal', or 'This power of attorney shall become effective upon the disability or incapacity of the principal', or similar words showing the intent of the principal that the authority conferred shall continue notwithstanding the subsequent disability or incapacity of the principal."

Therefore, the first requirement is that there be a written and signed document, and second, that the document contains words such as those above which clearly indicate that the principal intended the POA to be effective even after he or she became incapacitated. Although the language of the Uniform Act does not specifically state whether the document must also be notarized in order to be durable, the form recommended by the Uniform Law Commission has a space for the signature of a notary. Most states require POAs to be notarized to be durable, and for them to be effective for real estate transactions. It is recommended that your POA be notarized. Also, some states require witnesses to the principal's signature.

Advanced Directives (Living Wills)

Any healthcare professional will tell you that having an advanced directive (living will) may be the most important document you ever put together in your entire life. Having an advanced directive helps adult children, or any loved one, understand your wishes for the end of your life when you are no longer able to communicate those wishes yourself.

The term "advanced directive" refers to legal means by which individuals can express and, within certain limits, enforce their wishes regarding health care in the event that they become unconscious or otherwise mentally incapacitated. Common examples include living wills (which may direct families and physicians to withhold or withdraw life support if the person is terminally ill and for permanently unconscious) and durable powers of attorney (which appoint and invest third parties with full authority to make decisions regarding healthcare for incapacitated patients). When properly set up, these documents provide those who, in good faith, follow their provisions with protection from prosecution and civil suit.

A good elder law attorney (*www.naela.org*) can assist you and your family members draft an advanced directive, and most hospitals today will provide the forms and notaries for you upon admission to the hospital.

Five Wishes

One example of an advanced directive is called "Five Wishes". The Five Wishes document helps you express how you want to be treated if you are seriously ill and unable to speak for yourself. It is unique among all other living will and health agent forms because it looks to all of a person's needs: medical, personal, emotional and spiritual. Five Wishes also encourages discussing your wishes with your family and physician. Additional information can be found at *www.agingwithdignity.org*

Five Wishes Lets Your Family and Doctors Know:

- Which person you want to make health care decisions for you when you cannot make them.
- The kind of medical treatment you want or do not want.
- How comfortable you want to be.
- How you want people to treat you.
- What you want your loved ones to know.

Revocable Living Trust

This is a trust created by an individual (the trustor), and administered by another party (the trustee), while the trustor is still alive. The individual creating the living trust can be his or her own trustee while they are living and not incapacitated. Upon the individual's death, a successor trustee named in the trust will become the administrator. A living trust can be either revocable or irrevocable. At the time of death, a living trust avoids probate in court and therefore gets assets of the estate distributed much more quickly and with less cost than a will does. It also offers a higher level of confidentiality, as probate proceedings are a matter of public record. Additionally, trusts are usually harder to contest than wills.

On the downside, a living trust takes longer to put together than a will, and requires more ongoing maintenance. Although both a will and a living trust can be modified or revoked at any time before death, such changes are slightly more time-consuming for a living trust. Additionally, assets that a person wants to move to a living trust, such as real estate and bank or brokerage accounts, have to be re-titled in the name of the trust.

Irrevocable Trusts

An irrevocable trust is an arrangement in which the grantor departs with ownership and control of property. Usually this involves a gift of the property to the trust. The trust then stands as a separate taxable entity and pays tax on its accumulated income. Trusts typically receive a deduction for income that is distributed on a current basis. Because the grantor must permanently depart with the ownership and control of the property being transferred to an irrevocable trust, such a device has limited appeal to most taxpayers.

Homes that have been put into an irrevocable trust are generally not eligible for a reverse mortgage. An irrevocable trust is typically used in very advanced estate-planning strategies.

CHAPTER THIRTEEN

How to Use Medicaid to Pay for Long-Term Care

While Medicaid should be used as a last resort to pay for long-term care, there are two cases where this may be the only option for a family to protect assets. The first example is a married couple. In the case of a married couple, the federal law allows for a division of assets to occur at the time that either spouse enters a nursing home. Simply put, the couple is able to divide their assets by two and the healthy spouse, usually considered the community spouse, is able to keep half of the assets up to $119,220. Put another way, let's assume we have a couple, Mary, age 78, and her husband, Bill, age 82, with countable assets totaling $380,000. Even though when you divide the assets by two, you would expect that each spouse would be entitled to $190,000, the healthy spouse, i.e. community spouse, is only able to keep $119,220 in this example. The balance of $260,780 would need to be spent down to $2,000 before Medicaid will begin paying. (The amount in

Missouri is $999.99.) However, if the family is aware of the OBRA 93 (the Omnibus Reconciliation Act of 1993), they would learn that, actually, the healthy spouse can retain the $260,780 by converting this amount into the OBRA 93 Medicaid compliant annuity. While many individuals have annuities, this particular annuity is something that you would only come in contact with if you are in a long-term care crisis and are attempting to do Medicaid or Veterans planning. In order for an annuity to be Medicaid compliant it must be irrevocable, nonassignable, noncommutable, nontransferable and actuarially sound. When properly done, this planning will allow the healthy spouse to maintain 100 % of the assets by using the OBRA 93 Medicaid compliant annuity (See Exhibit 13.1).

Exhibit 13.1

Medicaid Spend-Down 101

ALL Assets from Both Spouses Fit into 1 of 3 Categories:

Exempt Assets	Countable Assets	Unavailable Assets
Principal Residence	Other Real Estate	OBRA '93 Compliant Annuity
Business Property	CD's, Checking, Savings, MM, $380,000	
One Car	Stocks, Bonds, Brokerage	
Personal Contents	Annuities	
Term Life Insurance	IRA	
$1,500 of Cash Value in Whole Life Insurance Policy	Life Insurance Cash Value	
Prepaid funeral	Mutual Funds	

TOTALS: *$380,000*

Illustration for Immediate Medicaid Qualification

Total Countable Assets.............. **$380,000**

Division of Assets................Divisible by 2

Each Spouse's Share of Assets.....**$190,000**

Maximum Amount of Countable Assets Community Spouse Can Keep is $119,220

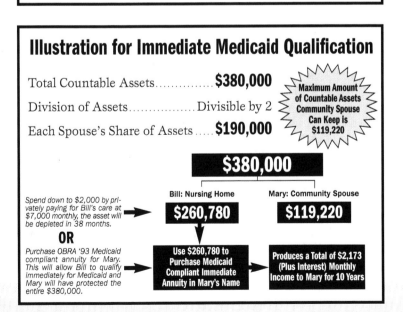

$380,000

Bill: Nursing Home	Mary: Community Spouse
$260,780	**$119,220**

Spend down to $2,000 by privately paying for Bill's care at $7,000 monthly, the asset will be depleted in 38 months.

OR

Purchase OBRA '93 Medicaid compliant annuity for Mary. This will allow Bill to qualify immediately for Medicaid and Mary will have protected the entire $380,000.

Use $260,780 to Purchase Medicaid Compliant Immediate Annuity in Mary's Name

Produces a Total of $2,173 (Plus Interest) Monthly Income to Mary for 10 Years

The case of a single individual using Medicaid as a long-term care planning strategy is a little more challenging. However, it may make sense to consider whether or not the family is concerned about making sure that there are adequate funds to pay for their parent's funeral expenses and other expenses that are not covered by Medicaid. Using a strategy commonly referred to as the "Half Loaf" strategy, an individual would transfer approximately 50 % of the assets to their children or possibly into an irrevocable trust. The other 50 % would be deposited into the OBRA 93 Medicaid compliant annuity. The income generated from the annuity, along with Social Security and pension income, would pay for the cost of care during the penalty period that was created by making a transfer of the other 50 %. Put another way, let's use Edith, age 80, who recently entered a nursing home where they have Medicaid beds available. Since Edith has an IRA worth $150,000, and an additional $150,000 in her money market and checking accounts she would be unable to qualify for Medicaid. However, if we transferred her $150,000 to a properly drafted irrevocable trust and the remaining balance of $150,000 IRA into an OBRA 93 Medicaid compliant annuity, the income from this IRA annuity, along with her Social Security and pension, would allow her to privately pay during the penalty that was created by transferring the other $150,000 into the trust. As a result, Edith would be eligible to receive Medicaid benefits after the penalty of only 31 months. The end result is that Edith has now protected half of her assets, or $150,000, for her future needs and the future of her children (See Exhibit 13.2).

Exhibit 13.2

Medicaid Spend Down 101

ALL Assets from Both Spouses Fit into 1 of 3 Categories:

Exempt Assets	Countable Assets	Unavailable Assets
Principal Residence	Other Real Estate	OBRA '93 Compliant Annuity
Business Property	CD's, Checking, Savings, MM, $150,000	
One Car	EE Bonds	
Personal Contents	Annuities	
Term Life Insurance	IRA – $150,000	
$1,500 of Cash Value in Whole Life Insurance Policy	Mutual Funds, Stocks, Bonds	
Prepaid funeral	Cash Value Life Insurance	

TOTALS: *$300,000*

Exhibit 13.2 continued on the next page …

Asset Protection Plan

Exhibit 13.2

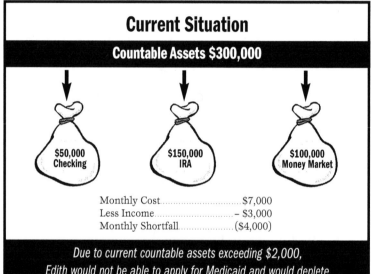

Current Situation

Countable Assets $300,000

$50,000
Checking

$150,000
IRA

$100,000
Money Market

Monthly Cost	$7,000
Less Income	– $3,000
Monthly Shortfall	($4,000)

*Due to current countable assets exceeding $2,000,
Edith would not be able to apply for Medicaid and would deplete
100% of assets in approximately 6 years.*

Asset Protection Plan

Exhibit 13.2

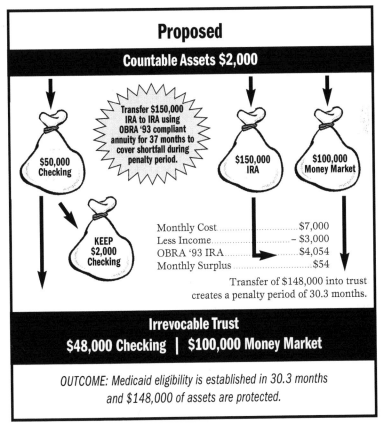

Proposed

Countable Assets $2,000

Transfer $150,000 IRA to IRA using OBRA '93 compliant annuity for 37 months to cover shortfall during penalty period.

$50,000 Checking

KEEP $2,000 Checking

$150,000 IRA

$100,000 Money Market

Monthly Cost	$7,000
Less Income	– $3,000
OBRA '93 IRA	$4,054
Monthly Surplus	$54

Transfer of $148,000 into trust creates a penalty period of 30.3 months.

Irrevocable Trust

$48,000 Checking | $100,000 Money Market

OUTCOME: Medicaid eligibility is established in 30.3 months and $148,000 of assets are protected.

CHAPTER FOURTEEN

How to Use Veterans Benefits to Pay for Long-Term Care

The Veterans' Administration offers a special pension with the Aid and Attendance (A&A) Benefit that is largely unknown. This Special Pension allows for Veterans and surviving spouses who require the regular attendance of another person to assist in eating, bathing, dressing, undressing, or taking care of the needs of nature to receive additional monetary benefits. It also includes individuals who are blind or a patient in a nursing home because of mental or physical incapacity. It is not a benefit for a person needing housekeeping or respite or part time care. Assisted care in an assisted-living facility also qualifies. This most important benefit is overlooked by many families with veterans or surviving spouses who need additional monies to help care for ailing parents or loved ones. This is a "pension benefit" and is not dependent upon service-related injuries for compensation. Many veterans who are in need of assistance qualify for this pension. Always seek professional advice when considering this type of assistance.

This special pension benefit addresses the needs of veterans and their surviving spouses who have non-service related disabilities and who require regular assistance with the activities of daily living.

In order for a veteran to qualify for this benefit, he or she must have served 90 days of active duty with one day of active service during a defined period of war.

The following are the VA's defined "periods of war":

* WWI: 4/16/1917 to 11/11/1918
* WWII: 12/7/1941 to 12/31/1946
* Korea: 6/25/1950 to 1/31/1955
* Vietnam: 8/5/1964 to 5/7/1975
* Persian Gulf: 8/2/90 to present

Income and liquid assets are also a determination of eligibility. Most people believe that if a single veteran has assets in his name below $50,000, or if a married couple has assets below $80,000, they may qualify. However, the reality is that the adjudicator, the person who approves claims at the VA, should apply an age-based analysis that takes into consideration the age of the veteran and/or surviving spouse, the amount of monthly income, and the cost of nonreimbursed medical expenses to determine the maximum amount of assets they can have in their name and still qualify. As a result, using the $80,000 number or $50,000 number may be problematic.

So the million-dollar question is, "What should the veteran do if their assets exceed the maximum amount determined by the age-based analysis?" One option is to take advantage of the fact that, unlike Medicaid, the VA currently has no five year look-back rule. Put another way, if a veteran or surviving spouse of a veteran has assets that exceed the age-based analysis amount, they could consider transferring assets to a properly drafted irrevocable trust. By doing so, assuming the rest of the planning has been done properly, they may be eligible for VA Aid and Attendance beginning the first day of the following month. A word of warning is that it is currently taking, in many cases, between 6-8 months to get a claim approved. In these cases, the VA does provide retroactive payment back to the first day of the month following the application (See Exhibit 14.1).

How Much Does VA Pay?

Aid and Attendance can help pay for care in the home, nursing home or assisted-living facility. A veteran is eligible for up to $1,794 per month, while a surviving spouse is eligible for up to $1,153 per month. A couple is eligible for up to $2,127 per month.

In many cases, if a person has a paid caregiver such as a nurse's aide, or they pay an assisted-living facility, those expenses impact so greatly on a person's net income that they will meet the criteria for the income level.

If a veteran or veteran's widow has cash assets above the limit, they are allowed to place those assets into certain investments in order to have them "sheltered." This sheltering does not have a penalty or "look-back period" associated with it. Proper asset sheltering for Aid and Attendance should be done under the supervision of a financial and legal Eldercare professional well versed in Medicaid planning. One could easily ruin the chances of ever getting Medicaid if the VA pension planning was done incorrectly.

With a little professional planning, many veterans and veterans' widows can receive pensions that make a significant difference in the amount of care they receive. After all, the reason for this particular pension is to assure that a veteran or veteran's widow does not live in a substandard environment in their old age. It takes a little work to apply for this pension, but anything worth having usually does.

Although you can apply on your own, it is best to seek the advice of a professional. There is no fee to apply and find out if you or a loved one is entitled to these services (See Exhibit 14.1).

Asset Protection Plan

Exhibit 14.1

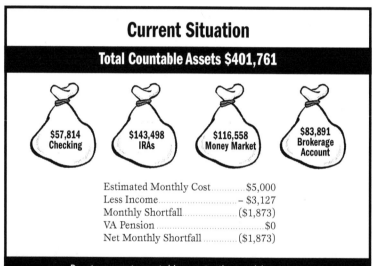

Current Situation

Total Countable Assets $401,761

$57,814
Checking

$143,498
IRAs

$116,558
Money Market

$83,891
Brokerage
Account

Estimated Monthly Cost............$5,000
Less Income................................ – $3,127
Monthly Shortfall.....................($1,873)
VA Pension.......................................$0
Net Monthly Shortfall............($1,873)

*Due to current countable assets, the surviving spouse
of the veteran would not currently be eligible
for Aid and Attendance pension benefits and would need to cover
the net monthly shortfall from income generated from assets.*

Asset Protection Plan

Exhibit 14.1

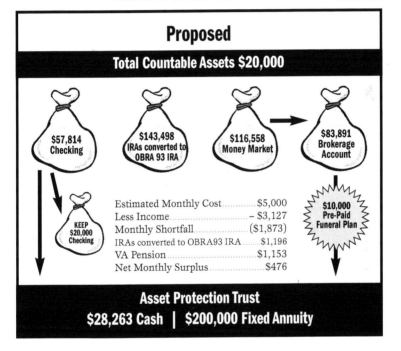

Proposed

Total Countable Assets $20,000

$57,814 Checking

$143,498 IRAs converted to OBRA 93 IRA

$116,558 Money Market

$83,891 Brokerage Account

KEEP $20,000 Checking

Estimated Monthly Cost.............$5,000
Less Income..............................– $3,127
Monthly Shortfall....................($1,873)
IRAs converted to OBRA93 IRA........$1,196
VA Pension...............................$1,153
Net Monthly Surplus....................$476

$10,000 Pre-Paid Funeral Plan

Asset Protection Trust
$28,263 Cash | $200,000 Fixed Annuity

SECTION FIVE

Finding Answers

CHAPTER FIFTEEN

Finding a Trusted Advisor Who Can Help

I f you are struggling with a long-term care crisis for an aging parent, an Eldercare financial plan will become your roadmap on how to pay for home care, assisted living, or nursing home costs in the most tax efficient, cost effective way possible. As an integral part of the plan, your financial professional should investigate government programs such as Medicaid and veterans benefits for qualifying veterans to further reduce the cost of out-of-pocket expenses for care.

Here is what you should expect from a qualified financial professional who can walk you through the right process:

1. A professional who will clearly define your loved one's care needs and costs.

2. Comprehensive analysis and evaluation of all sources of income, expenses, cash flow, taxes, current asset allocation, economic variables, and health/longevity risks.

3. Analysis of the facts and creation of a written comprehensive plan in a language that you can understand.

4. Implementation of plan: In an effort to achieve the best results from the Eldercare financial plan, the professional will coordinate their efforts with elder law attorneys who will help you with the application for Medicaid, and veteran benefits when appropriate. Upon implementation of the plan, they should carefully monitor it, and communicate with you on a regular basis through periodic reviews and quarterly performance reports. Your advisor should have considerable experience in long-term care planning.

Registered Investment Advisors— Getting the Right Advice

What Is an Investment Advisor?

An investment advisor is an individual or a firm that is in the business of giving advice about securities to clients. For instance, individuals or firms that receive compensation for giving advice on investing in stocks, bonds, mutual funds, or exchange traded funds are investment advisors. Some investment advisors manage portfolios of securities.

What Is the Difference between an Investment Advisor and a Financial Planner?

Most financial planners are investment advisors, but not all investment advisors are financial planners. Some financial planners assess every aspect of your financial life—including savings, investments, insurance, taxes, retirement, and estate planning—and help you develop a detailed strategy or financial plan for meeting all your financial goals.

Others call themselves financial planners, but they may only be able to recommend that you invest in a narrow range of products, and sometimes products that are not securities.

Before you hire any financial professional, you should know exactly what services you need, what services the professional can deliver, any limitations on what they can recommend, what services you are paying for, how much those services cost, and how the advisor or planner gets paid.

What Questions Should I Ask When Choosing an Investment Advisor or Financial Planner?

Here are some of the questions you should always ask when hiring any financial professional:

- What experience do you have, especially with people in my circumstances?

- Where did you go to school? What is your recent employment history?

- What licenses do you hold? Are you registered with the SEC, a state, or the Financial Industry Regulatory Authority (FINRA)?

- What products and services do you offer?

- Can you only recommend a limited number of products or services to me? If so, why?

- How are you paid for your services? What is your usual hourly rate, flat fee, or commission?

- Have you ever been disciplined by any government regulator for unethical or improper conduct or been sued by a client who was not happy with the work you did?

- For registered investment advisors, will you send me a copy of both parts of your Form ADV? Form ADV is divided into two parts. The first discloses specific information about a Registered Investment Advisor (RIA) that is important to regulators—name, number of employees, form of organization, nature of business, etc. The second part acts as a disclosure document for clients of the business and includes information such as the services provided and fees charged —whether the investment advisor acts as a broker-dealer and transacts securities, and so on.

Be sure to meet potential advisors "face to face" to make sure you get along. And remember: there are many types of individuals who can help you develop a personal financial plan and manage your hard-earned money. The most important thing is that you know your financial goals, have a plan in place, and check out the professional you choose with your securities regulator.

How Do Investment Advisors Get Paid?

Before you hire any financial professional—whether it is a stockbroker, a financial planner, or an investment advisor— you should always find out and make sure you understand how that person gets paid. Investment advisors generally are paid in any of the following ways:

* A percentage of the value of the assets they manage for you,
* An hourly fee for the time they spend working for you,
* A fixed fee,
* A commission on the securities they sell (if the advisor is also a broker-dealer),
* Some combination of the above.

Each compensation method has potential benefits and possible drawbacks depending on your individual needs. Ask the investment advisors you interview to explain the differences to you before you do business with them, and get several opinions before making your decision. Also, ask if the fee is negotiable.

Elder Law Attorneys

Aging adults and their family members face certain challenging legal issues. Issues such as legal matters, financial matters, and care planning can be complicated for seniors, as well as for their family. Once again, expert legal help is often the key to solving many problems and avoiding future complexities. It is important to be able to identify a competent elder law attorney who can assist the family in a timely and professional manner. Consumers should be cautious and check credentials thoroughly.

The leading national organization of elder law attorneys is the National Academy of Elder Law Attorneys (NAELA), on the web at: *www.naela.org*. Membership is open to any lawyer, but the membership does show that at least the attorney has some interest in the field. Other sources to consider are referrals from family and friends, and referrals from other professionals such as social workers and medical professionals who work in long-term care. Ask the attorney how many nursing-home cases they handle each month. It is likely that the attorney who does four Medicaid cases per month is more up to date than the attorney who does four per year.

Legal problems that affect the elderly are growing in number. Our laws and regulations are becoming more complex. Actions taken by older people with regard to a single matter may have unintended legal effects. It is important for attorneys dealing with seniors to have a broad understanding of the laws that may have an impact on a given situation, to avoid future problems.

Elder law attorneys can help with:

- trusts
- wills
- durable powers of attorney

* Medicaid and VA benefits
* advanced medical directives
* other important legal issues and documents

Geriatric Care Managers as a Resource

When faced with decisions regarding long-term care for an aging loved one, a geriatric care manager may be one of the best private resources in your area. A geriatric care manager has extensive knowledge of all local resources related to aging and caregiving, as well as family and personal issues and concerns.

Geriatric care managers can be located nationwide. They assist with coordination of care for aging and disabled adults. This service is provided in a series of steps including initial assessment, care plan development, implementation of services, and quality-of-care monitoring. Geriatric care managers are typically nurses, social workers, gerontologists, physical therapists, occupational therapists, or other social service professionals.

The "care management" process can improve the quality of life not only for the aging adult, but also for the caregivers and family members involved. The service is very personalized and utilizes the same principles of "case management."

Most geriatric care managers are available to the family and client 24 hours per day, 7 days per week. The ultimate goal is to keep the aging adult in the home for as long as **safely** possible. In-home care can be arranged at any level of need to accommodate the client and the family. Geriatric care managers often will be asked to arrange other services for the client, such as bill paying, housekeeping, lawn care, transportation to appointments, grocery shopping, meal delivery, and personal care.

When the client is in need of transition to alternative living arrangements, such as a nursing home, assisted living, or even an independent retirement community, the care manager can often recommend the best facilities to meet the client's financial needs.

Geriatric care management is truly a holistic approach to caring for the aging adult. All resources available are utilized to assist families when long-term care is needed.

Care managers are also often asked to troubleshoot quality concerns with nursing homes and home-care agencies. Their level of professionalism and knowledge of the local regulations and laws are of great value to the family. They are considered "advocates" for the elderly.

Geriatric care management is paid for privately by client and family members. Medicare and Medicaid do not cover these services. However, long-term care insurance does cover some or all of the care management fee.

Most geriatric care managers belong to the National Association of Professional Geriatric Care Managers. In order to find a care manager in your area, you can search for one through their website at *www.caremanager.org.*

Recommendations for Choosing a Geriatric Care Manager

Choosing a geriatric care manager is much like choosing any other professional that you and your family would be working with closely.

- Look for a member of the National Association of Professional Geriatric Care Managers. These members have met certain criteria regarding education and experience in health sciences and social service.

- Ask for references.

- Ask for literature about their company, years of practice, websites, and biography.

- Check with the Better Business Bureau.

- Ask about fees, contracts, and extra charges like mileage or phone calls.

- Be sure you understand what services they provide and their on-call schedule. Will they be available 24 hours a day?

- Remember that a geriatric care manager becomes your "eyes and ears," especially when you live some distance from your parents. Ask them about their process and their communication schedule (Will they report daily, weekly, or monthly?). Is the primary communication via telephone or email?

- Communicate any concerns immediately, and work together as a team to accomplish the ultimate goal, which is keeping your loved one safe and well cared for.

My Parent Doesn't Want Any Help, What Should I Do?

Perhaps you have noticed that Mom or Dad is not bathing regularly, or the bills are not being paid, or the house is uncharacteristically messy. Maybe they seem to forget directions from one location to another, or even worse, they have had a car accident, or report falling in the home when no one was around to help them. Often adult children of aging parents notice changes in their loved ones, and when the aging adult is confronted with the facts, they say, "Oh everything is fine, I don't need any help, don't worry about me!"

The loss of independence and choice is something no one wants to face. Having one's own children tell them what to do or how to live their lives is uncomfortable at best. Many aging adults are also very private about their financial matters, and will not discuss income, expenses, or assets with adult children.

How Does an Adult Child Start That Conversation with Their Parents?

There is not a one-size-fits-all answer. Below are some tips that might help the process along.

- Choose an appropriate time and place. Avoid large family gatherings, holidays, birthdays, and other celebrations. A quiet location, in their home or yours, might be more comfortable.

- Avoid blaming or accusing. Instead, redirect the conversation by telling your parent how YOU feel. For example, "Mom, I find myself worrying about you a lot these days, and I would like to tell you why I am feeling this way."

- Talk to a geriatric care manager in your area for some good advice on how to approach your parent's specific needs. That care manager has helped family members have this kind of conversation hundreds of times throughout their career. They are full of helpful hints and tips.

- If you decide to seek the services of a geriatric care manager, ask them about their approach when it comes to dealing with difficult clients or clients who may not perceive a need for services.

- Advice for adult children when approaching their parents about setting up an evaluation might include telling their parents, "I know you don't want me to worry about you, and I only want the best for you. Having this professional come over and talk to us would really make me feel better. If you would agree to talk with her, we can look at her recommendations together and see if any of them make sense. Is that fair?"

- Remember that having a third party, who is not a family member and is completely objective, can help the senior see things from a different point of view. They feel like they are getting some professional advice as opposed to opinions from their children.

- Finally, if the senior is truly not living safely, a geriatric care manager can let the senior know that they need to make some choices about their care or living arrangements NOW, before someone else has to make that decision for them later. Of course, this is done with professionalism, courtesy, compassion and caring.

Conclusion

I t comes as no surprise to anyone that the family dynamic in America has changed over the years. Seniors often worry about outliving their money and what would happen if they ever really did need expensive long-term care!? Economics demand that most of us of "working age" have two-income families, and we find ourselves busy with our children's extra-curricular activities. Furthermore, most of us with aging family members have had that thought in the back of our minds more than once— "What are we going to do with/for Mom and Dad when the time comes where they can no longer care for themselves?"

Most seniors today live independently or at home with some form of assistance coming in to attend to their needs. Only 20% of seniors who need care are actually in nursing homes, while 80% are cared for in a home-like setting.

Every stage of our lives brings with it changes, fears, obstacles, questions, wonders, opportunities, happy times, and not-so-happy times. Seniors will tell you that their greatest fears are losing their autonomy, dignity, respect, and independence. Above all else, they are afraid of outliving their money and being put in a nursing home for their remaining days.

Everyone wants to live at home for life. I have yet to meet an aging adult who will tell you that they ultimately prefer to live in a nursing home. For some the process is inevitable.

There may come a time for many of us when care at home becomes impossible, mainly for safety or economic reasons.

Although in-home care is less costly than nursing-home care, 24/7 in-home care is difficult for most families to afford to pay for privately. Long-term care insurance is one solution to keeping seniors safe and at home for longer periods of time. Planning ahead for long-term care has never been a more important concept. However for some seniors and their families, it is either too late (poor health), or too expensive to afford long-term care insurance.

There are other solutions and ways to manage the crisis of long-term care needs for seniors. There are ways that seniors can help themselves, and families can rest easier knowing that Mom and Dad will be taken care of with the dignity and respect they deserve. All of this can now happen at home for much longer periods of time. Education empowers consumers to remain independent for as long as possible. Talk with each other about long-term care issues and concerns in your family before a crisis happens.

Resources

The following listings are resources available to seniors and their family members nationwide.

Reverse Mortgage Information and Services

National Reverse Mortgage Lenders Association
1400 16th St., NW
Suite 420
Washington, DC 20036
202.939.1760
www.nrmlaonline.org

Long-Term Care Insurance/ Health Insurance

Weiss Ratings, Inc.
4176 Burns Road
Palm Beach Gardens, FL 33410
800.289.9222
www.weissratings.com
Financial ratings on long-term care insurance companies can be found here.

National Association of Insurance Commissioners—NAIC
Hall of States
444 North Capitol Street, NW
Suite 701
Washington, DC 20001-1512
202.624.7790 (Voice)
www.naic.org

American Association of Health Plans
601 Pennsylvania Avenue NW
South Building
Suite 500
Washington, DC 20004
www.ahip.org

American Association of Long-Term Care Insurance
AALTCI
3835 E. Thousand Oaks Blvd. Suite 336
Westlake Village, CA   91362
818.597.3227
www.aaltci.org

The Center for Long-Term Care Reform
2212 Queen Anne Ave North #110
Seattle, WA 98109
206.283.7036
www.centerltc.org

Government Agencies of Interest

Department of Veterans Affairs (VA)
810 Vermont Ave. NW
Washington, DC 20420
800.827.1000
www.va.gov

Paralyzed Veterans of America (PVA)
Veterans Benefits Dept.
801 18th St., NW
Washington, DC 20006
800.424.8200
www.pva.org

Centers for Medicare & Medicaid Services (CMS)
Region VII
Richard Bolling Federal Building, Room 235
601 East 12th Street
Kansas City, Missouri 64106
800.MEDICARE
www.medicare.gov

Centers for Medicare and Medicaid Services (CMS),
formerly the Health Care Financing Administration—CMS
200 Independence Avenue, SW
Room 303-D
Washington, DC 20201
877.267.2323 (Voice – Toll-free)
question@cms.gov
www.cms.gov

Area Agencies on Aging
Eldercare Locator
927 15th St. NW, 6th Floor
Washington, DC 20005
Eldercare Locator: 800.677.1116
www.n4a.org
www.eldercare.gov

National Institute on Aging
www.nia-nih.gov

National Council on Aging
1901 L Street, N.W., 4th floor
Washington, D.C. 20036
Phone: 202.479.1200
TDD: 202.479.6674
info@ncoa.org
www.ncoa.org

Legal Resources

Commission on Legal Problems of the Elderly
www.abanet.org/elderly

National Academy of Elder Law Attorneys
1604 N Country Club Road
Tucson, AZ 85716 USA
www.naela.org

SeniorLaw
www.seniorlaw.com

Caregiver Resources: Home Care and Adult Day Care

National Adult Day Services Association, Inc.
8201 Greensboro Drive, Suite 300
McLean, Virginia 22102
Toll Free Phone: 866.890.7357 or 703.610.9035
info@nadsa.org
www.nadsa.org

National Association for Home Care
228 7th Street, SE
Washington, DC 20003
202.547.7424
www.nahc.org

ABLEDATA—Assistive Devices
8630 Fenton Street, Suite 930
Silver Spring, MD 20910
Phone: 800.227.0216
TTY: 301.608.8912
www.abledata.com

Meals on Wheels Association of America
www.mowaa.org

Caregiver Resources: Hospice

Partnership For Caring
1620 Eye Street NW, Suite 202,
Washington, DC 20006
Phone: 202.296.8071
Hotline: 800.989.9455
www.caringinfo.org

Hospice Foundation of America
2001 S St. NW #300
Washington DC 20009
Phone: 800.854.3402
www.hospicefoundation.org

National Hospice & Palliative Care Organization (NHPCO)
1700 Diagonal Road, Suite 625
Alexandria, Virginia 22314
Phone: 703.837.1500
The NHPCO Helpline: 800.658.8898
www.nhpco.org

Resources for Caregivers: Housing

The Assisted Living Federation of America
11200 Waples Mill Rd
Suite 150
Fairfax, VA 22030
Phone: 703.691.8100
info@alfa.org
www.alfa.org

National Shared Housing Resource Center
www.nationalsharedhousing.org

National Center for Assisted Living—NCAL
1201 L Street, NW
Washington, DC 20005
Phone: 202.842.4444
www.ncal.org

Leading Age
2519 Connecticut Ave. NW
Washington, DC 20008
Phone: 800.508.9442
www.leadingage.org

The Eden Alternative™
www.edenalt.com

Caregiver Resources: Geriatric Care Management

Aging Life Care Association
3275 W. Ina Road
Suite 130
Tucson, AZ 85741
www.aginglifecare.org

Caregiver Resources: Medications

American Pharmacists Association
2215 Constitution Avenue, NW
Washington, DC 20037
Phone: 202.628.4410
www.pharmacist.com

Center Watch—Clinical Drug Trials Listings
www.centerwatch.com

MEDLINEplus
www.nlm.nih.gov/medlineplus

Caregiver Resources: Finding Doctors

American Medical Association—AMA
515 North State Street
Chicago, IL 60610
Phone: 312.464.4818
amalibrary@ama-assn.org
www.ama-assn.org

Gerontological Society of America
www.geron.org

Caregiver Resources:
Caregiver Organizations and Support

Caregiver Action Network
1130 Connecticut Avenue NW, #300
Washington, DC 20036
Phone: 202.454.3970
www.caregiveraction.org

Well Spouse Foundation
63 West Main Street—Suite H
Freehold, NJ 07728
Phone: 800.838.0879
www.wellspouse.org

Other Caregiver Sites of Interest

www.caregiving.com

www.caregiver.com

www.carescout.com

http://griefnet.org

Senior Advocacy and Interest Groups

National Consumers League
1701 K Street, NW, Suite 1200
Washington, DC 20006
Phone: 202.835.3323
www.natlconsumersleague.org

Families USA
www.familiesusa.org

ElderWeb
www.elderweb.com

United Seniors Health Council—USHC
409 3rd St., SW, Suite 200
Washington, DC 20024
Phone: 202.479.6673
www.unitedseniorshealth.org

American Health Care Association
1201 L Street, N.W., Washington, DC 20005
Phone: 202.842.4444
www.ahca.org

Alliance for Retired Americans
888 16th St., N.W.
Suite 520
Washington, D.C. 20006
Phone: 888.373.6497
www.retiredamericans.org

American Society on Aging—ASA
833 Market Street
Suite 511
San Francisco, CA 94103
415.974.9600
info@asaging.org
www.asaging.org

Alliance for Aging Research
2021 K Street, NW
Suite 305
Washington, DC 20006
Phone: 800.639.2421
info@agingresearch.org
www.agingresearch.org

AARP
www.aarp.org

Benefits Check-Up
www.benefitscheckup.org

Miscellaneous Sites of Interest

Mayo Clinic
www.mayohealth.org

On Health
www.webmd.com

Specific Disease Processes and Organizations On-Line:

National Alzheimer's Association
www.alz.org

Alzheimer's Research Forum
www.alzforum.org

American Cancer Society
www.cancer.org

American Diabetes Association
www.diabetes.org

American Heart Association
www.americanheart.org

American Stroke Association
A Division of American Heart Association
7272 Greenville Avenue
Dallas, TX 75231
888.4STROKE
strokeassociation@heart.org
www.strokeassociation.org

Arthritis Foundation
www.arthritis.org

National Organization for Rare Disorders
www.rarediseases.org

National Association for Continence
www.nafc.org

National Osteoporosis Foundation
www.nof.org

National Sleep Foundation
www.sleepfoundation.org

Parkinson's Resource Organization
www.parkinsonsresource.org

Hearing Loss Association of America
www.hearingloss.com

Lighthouse Guild
111 East 50th Street
New York, NY 10022
Phone:800.254.4422
www.lighthouseguild.org